WordPerfect ®

Lessons—A Classroom Workbook

WordPerfect Corporation, 288 West Center Street, Orem, Utah 84057 U.S.A.,
Telephone: (801) 225-5000, Telex: 820618 WPC, FAX: (801) 227-4288

ISBN 1-55692-003-2

Table of Contents

Introduction

Learning WordPerfect is a classroom supplement to the WordPerfect word processing package. It contains a series of lessons that take you step-by-step through various word processing tasks. Each of the lessons in this supplement begins with a brief introduction and ends with an illustration of the finished product.

As you work through lessons, do not become discouraged if you get lost or do not completely understand why the screen does what it does. You can always start a lesson over by clearing the screen.

> F7, N, ↵ Clear the screen.

Before beginning the lessons, read through this Introduction to learn some basics about your keyboard, template, and the conventions we use throughout the supplement. At the end of the Introduction is a brief preview of WordPerfect that teaches you how to start the program, perform some basic editing tasks, and exit.

The lessons are divided into two parts. The *Fundamentals* unit concentrates on formatting and editing skills, introducing you to most of WordPerfect's features. The *Special Features* unit contains some more advanced applications, including a few more WordPerfect features.

The Template

The keyboard template is WordPerfect's menu. Place the template on the keyboard as shown in the photograph.

Colors

The template is color coded.

Black	Press the function key.
Blue	Hold down Alt and press the function key.
Green	Hold down Shift and press the function key.
Red	Hold down Ctrl and press the function key.

Function keys

WordPerfect uses some keys on your keyboard to perform its many features. These function keys work in different ways. Some, such as Bold and Underline, simply toggle a feature on and off. Others, such as Print and Footnote, display a menu of choices. Still others begin a feature, such as Center or Indent, that is ended when the Enter key is pressed. The Save and Retrieve features, on the other hand, require that a filename be entered.

When you are asked to press a number key (0-9) in response to a menu of choices, use the numbers at the top of the keyboard instead of those on the number pad.

Six keys to know

You should be familiar with the following six keys before starting any of the lessons.

Num Lock

Some keyboards have a separate 10-key number pad that is also used for cursor control in WordPerfect. Press the Num Lock key (or its equivalent) once for numbers; press it again for cursor control. The "Pos" message at the bottom of the screen flashes when this key is on.

Help

Press this key for information about each WordPerfect feature. A feature-key reference can also be displayed.

Backspace

This key is used to erase mistakes as you type.

Enter (Return)

Use this key to end a short line of text or to send a command to the computer. For example, to retrieve or save a file, you must type a filename and then press this key.

Cancel

Use this key to back out of features that display a message on the status line. For example, the Exit, Save, Retrieve, Block, and Search prompts can all be canceled by striking this key once or twice. The Cancel key also restores text that has been erased by any of the delete keys.

Exit

Use this key to save a document, then clear the screen or get out of WordPerfect. This key also lets you leave menus such as Print, Page Format, and Select Printers. Use the Enter key when you finish typing a header, footer, footnote, or endnote.

Conventions

The following words have specific meanings and are used throughout the lessons.

TYPE	Type the bolded characters.
ENTER	Type the bolded characters, then press the Enter key.
MOVE	Move the cursor to the indicated place.
BLOCK	Define a block of text.
INSERT	Insert the given diskette into the specified drive.
REPLACE	Remove the diskette from the indicated drive and replace it with the given diskette.

Keys may appear by themselves, with another key, or as a series of keys. If keys in a series are *not* separated by commas, hold down the first key while quickly tapping the second.

F8	Tap the key.
Alt F8	Hold down the Alt key, then tap the F8 key.
Alt F8 , 1	Hold down the Alt key, tap the F8 key, release both keys, then type 1.
F7 , N , ↵	Tap the F7 key, type **n**, then tap the Enter key.

Start WordPerfect

How you start WordPerfect depends on whether you are using a computer with two diskette drives or a hard disk.

Two diskette drives

From the DOS prompt (A>):

INSERT The WordPerfect diskette into drive A.

INSERT The Learning diskette into drive B.

ENTER **b:** to change the default drive to B.

ENTER **a:wp** to start WordPerfect.

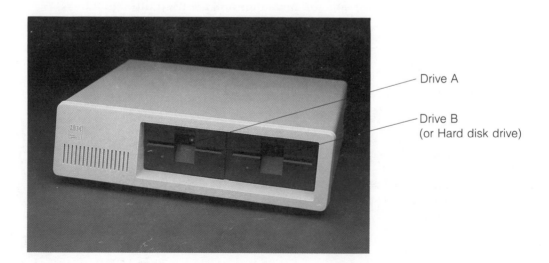

Drive A

Drive B
(or Hard disk drive)

Hard disk

Because of the variety of ways WordPerfect can be installed on a hard disk, consult the WordPerfect manual or your instructor for directions.

Clean screen

Starting WordPerfect is like rolling a clean sheet of paper into a typewriter with margins and spacing already set.

A help screen appears at startup time until printers are selected. Press any key to display a blank WordPerfect screen.

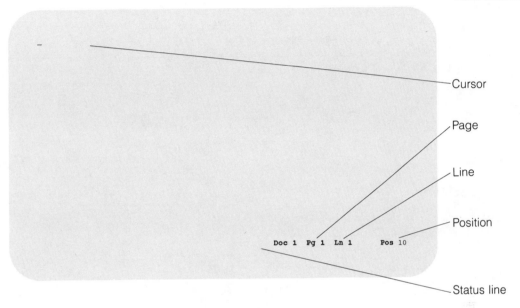

Cursor

Page

Line

Position

Doc 1 Pg 1 Ln 1   Pos 10

Status line

Cursor

The blinking dash or *cursor* points like a finger to your position on the page. The message at the bottom of the screen tells you the exact location of the cursor at all times.

Status line

Besides cursor position, this line also displays menus, messages, and warnings from WordPerfect and DOS.

After a document has been saved, the document name (including full pathname) is also displayed on the left-hand side of the status line. The document name may be temporarily replaced by such messages as "Typeover," "Block on," "Macro Def," etc.

Preview WordPerfect

During this preview, you will type, edit, and print a few paragraphs of text. Some fundamentals of WordPerfect are introduced here.

Begin by typing the following paragraph without pressing the Enter key. Use the Backspace key to erase mistakes as you type.

TYPE **Bears have been searching for food in campgrounds since the tourist season started. For this reason, we are increasing patrols for the next few weeks.**

```
Bears have been searching for food in campgrounds since the
tourist season started.  For this reason, we are increasing
patrols for the next few weeks._




                                        Doc 1  Pg 1  Ln 3      Pos 41
```

Now, change the format by inserting a tab, then edit the paragraph.

MOVE To the "B" in the word "Bears."

[Tab] Insert a Tab, and the cursor moves one tab stop to the right.

Use the Arrow keys to move the cursor.

MOVE To the "f" in the word "food."

TYPE **Chinese take-out**

[Space Bar] Insert space between "take-out" and "food."

[Home] , [Home] , [↓] Move to the bottom of the document.

The end of the paragraph is the bottom of the document. The cursor moves only through text and codes—it will not move through *nothing*.

TYPE Two spaces and finish the paragraph with two or three sentences of your own invention. (If you can't think of anything, just type this paragraph.)

MOVE To the beginning of the first word of the text you just typed.

6   Introduction

⏎ Press 2 times to return the cursor (and any text to the right of the cursor) to the next line and add a blank line.

Tab Insert a Tab to indent the first line of the new paragraph.

Ctrl F3 Press 2 times to reformat the screen.

```
     Bears have been searching for Chinese take-out food in
campgrounds since the tourist season started.  For this reason,
we are increasing patrols for the next few weeks.

     There are many large trees available for your use in the
event of an emergency.  It is recommended, however, that all
campers immediately dispose of any receptacles of soy sauce,
sweet and sour sauce, or fortune cookies.
```

It was nice to view the text as two paragraphs, but it doesn't look right. Return the second paragraph to its original place.

[Back-space] Press 3 times to create a single paragraph.

```
        Bears have been searching for Chinese take-out food in
campgrounds since the tourist season started.  For this reason,
we are increasing patrols for the next few weeks.  There are many
large trees available for your use in the event of an emergency.
It is recommended, however, that all campers immediately dispose
of any receptacles of soy sauce, sweet and sour sauce, or fortune
cookies.




                                     Doc 1  Pg 1  Ln 3       Pos 61
```

The Help key displays information about each feature. Before using the Center key, read about it in the Help screen.

[F3] Select the Help feature, and read the first Help screen.

[C] Find out where the Center key is located.

[Shift] [F6] Select the keys that correspond to the Center feature, then read about the Center key.

[Space Bar] Return to your paragraph.

Now, type a centered title.

[Home] , [Home] , [↑] Move to the top of the document.

[↵] Press 2 times to return the cursor to the next line and add a blank line.

[↑] Press 2 times to move back to the top of the document.

[Shift] [F6] Turn on centering. A center code that you cannot see has been placed in the text.

TYPE **"Bears"**

If you decide not to center the title after all, look at the Reveal Codes screen to find exactly where you placed the Center code.

Alt F3 Display the Reveal Codes screen.

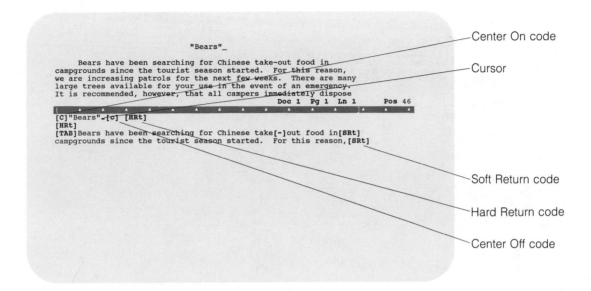

Center On code

Cursor

Soft Return code

Hard Return code

Center Off code

MOVE To the right of the Center On code.

Back-space Delete the Center code [C].

You can cancel centering by deleting either the Center On or Center Off code. The partner code will automatically be deleted.

Exit the Reveal Codes screen and return to the normal screen. With the Center code gone, the title should now be at the left margin.

```
"Bears"

     Bears have been searching for Chinese take-out food in
campgrounds since the tourist season started.  For this reason,
we are increasing patrols for the next few weeks. There are many
large trees available for your use in the event of an emergency.
It is recommended, however, that all campers immediately dispose
of any receptacles of soy sauce, sweet and sour sauce, or fortune
cookies.




                                    Doc 1  Pg 1  Ln 1      Pos 10
```

Page print

If your computer is connected to a printer which has been installed in WordPerfect, you can print the document you have created. If not, skip to "Save and exit."

 Select the *Page* option on the Print menu. Your document begins to print.

If your printer is set for Hand-fed forms, roll a sheet of paper into the printer, press the Print key, type 4 (Printer Control) and type g (go) to start printing.

"Bears"

Bears have been searching for Chinese take-out food in campgrounds since the tourist season started. For this reason, we are increasing patrols for the next few weeks. There are many large trees available, however, in the event of an emergency. It is recommended, however, that all campers immediately dispose of any receptacles of soy sauce, sweet and sour sauce, or fortune cookies.

Unless there is more than one page, "Full Text" and "Page" print do the same thing.

If the printer does not print, and you have installed WordPerfect and selected your printer, consult the WordPerfect user's manual or your instructor.

Save and exit

To end this preview lesson, save the document you have created, then exit WordPerfect. You must exit using the Exit key before turning off the computer.

F7 Select the Exit feature. You are asked if you want to save the document on the screen.

Y Answer "yes" to save the document.

ENTER **bears** as the filename. The document on the screen is saved in a file on disk called BEARS.

*Press the Enter key after typing **bears**.*

Y Answer "yes" to exit WordPerfect.

When you see the DOS prompt (A>, B>, etc.) at the bottom of the screen, you have exited WordPerfect.

You may now turn off your computer or load another program.

Fundamentals

Typing

In this lesson, you type a letter that confirms a reservation at Lone Pine National Park. When you finish, you print the letter, save it on your disk, then clear the screen.

While working through the lesson, you learn the following facts about WordPerfect's features:

- Backspace deletes to the left.
- Center centers a line of text.
- Bold and Underline highlight text.
- Caps Lock shifts the letters on your keyboard to uppercase.
- Word Wrap automatically returns the cursor to the left margin.
- Print lets you print the document on the screen.
- Exit clears your screen.

The skills you learn in this lesson can be used for

- Business letters.
- Letters of introduction.
- Letters to friends.
- Most correspondence.

1.1 Center, bold, and underline

You begin the letter by centering, bolding, and underlining a heading.

Shift F6 Turn on centering. The cursor moves to the center of the screen.

F6 Turn on bolding. Notice that the number next to "Pos" on the status line is bolded when the Bold feature is on.

F8 Turn on underlining also. Notice that the number next to "Pos" on the status line is underlined when the Underline feature is on.

TYPE **Lone Pine National Park**

Use the Backspace key to erase mistakes.

If you have a color or graphics monitor, underlined text is displayed as a separate color or in reverse video.

F6 Turn off bolding.

F8   Turn off underlining.

↵   Press 2 times to end centering and return the cursor to the next line, then add a blank line.

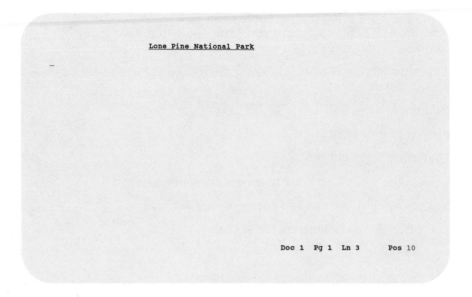

                      Lone Pine National Park

Doc 1 Pg 1 Ln 3   Pos 10

1.2   Caps Lock

The Caps Lock key lets you type uppercase letters without using the Shift key.

Caps Lock   Begin typing uppercase letters. Notice that the "Pos" at the bottom of the screen changes to "POS" as an indicator that you have pressed the Caps Lock key.

If you want to type a lowercase letter while using the Caps Lock feature, hold down the Shift key and tap the letter you want.

TYPE   **reservation confirmation**

Caps Lock   End typing uppercase letters. "POS" changes back to "Pos."

↵   Press 2 times to return the cursor to the next line and add a blank line.

If "Lone Pine National Park" does not appear brighter than "RESERVATION CONFIRMATION" on your screen, use the knob(s) on your monitor to adjust the brightness and contrast.

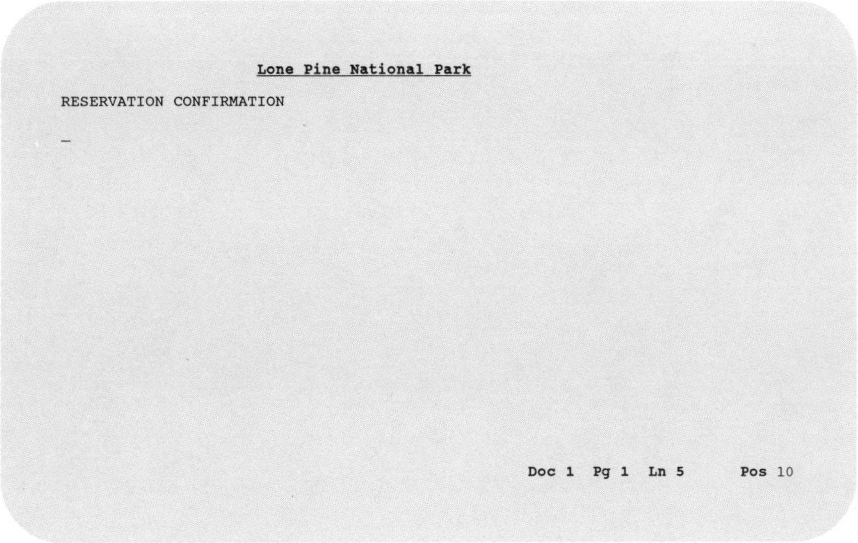

```
                    Lone Pine National Park

RESERVATION CONFIRMATION

_




                                      Doc 1  Pg 1  Ln 5     Pos 10
```

1.3 Address and salutation

Continue the letter by typing the address and salutation, using the Enter key to end each line and add blank lines.

TYPE **Frank D. Edwards**

⏎ Return the cursor to the next line.

TYPE **2345 N. Quail Road**

⏎ Return the cursor to the next line.

TYPE **Birdseye, Utah 84666**

⏎ Press 2 times to return the cursor to the next line and add a blank line.

TYPE **Dear Mr. Edwards,**

⌨ Press 2 times to return the cursor to the next line and add a blank line.

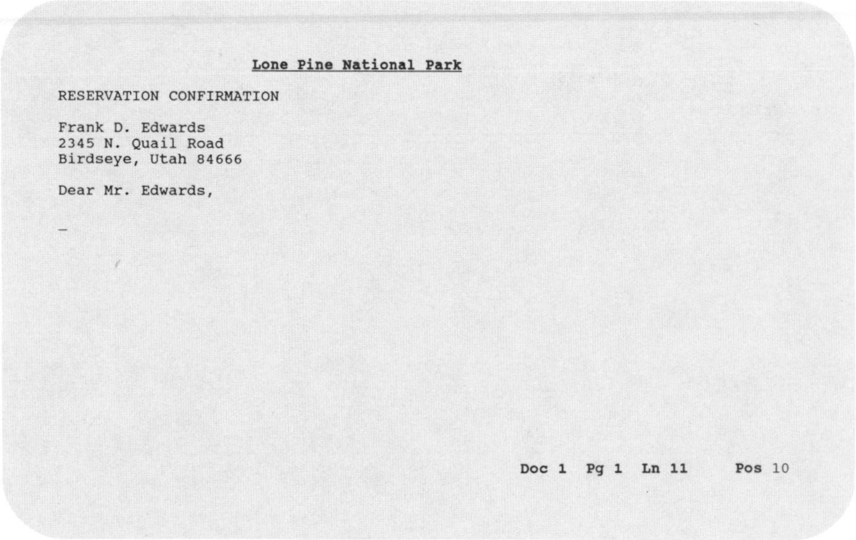

```
                    Lone Pine National Park
RESERVATION CONFIRMATION

Frank D. Edwards
2345 N. Quail Road
Birdseye, Utah 84666

Dear Mr. Edwards,

_




                                          Doc 1  Pg 1  Ln 11     Pos 10
```

1.4 Word Wrap

Now, type the body of the letter. As you type, let the automatic Word Wrap feature wrap lines within each paragraph. Use the Enter key only to end the last line of a paragraph.

If habit makes you press the Enter key prematurely, press the Backspace key to take back that action.

Tab Insert a Tab, and the cursor moves one tab stop to the right.

Lesson 3 details how to change tab stop positions.

TYPE **This letter is a confirmation of your request for a traditional log cabin.**

⌨ Press 2 times to return the cursor to the next line and add a blank line.

Tab Insert a Tab, and the cursor moves one tab stop to the right.

TYPE **The Mary Todd Lincoln Cabin has been reserved in your name for the week of June 10-17, 1984. The cabin includes three bedrooms, a full kitchen, large parlor, and hot tub. Limousine Service is also available at no extra charge.**

⏎ Press 2 times to return the cursor to the next line and add a blank line.

```
                        Lone Pine National Park

RESERVATION CONFIRMATION

Frank D. Edwards
2345 N. Quail Road
Birdseye, Utah 84666

Dear Mr. Edwards,

     This letter is a confirmation of your request for a
traditional log cabin.

     The Mary Todd Lincoln Cabin has been reserved in your name
for the week of June 10-17, 1984.  The cabin includes three
bedrooms, a full kitchen, large parlor, and a hot tub.  Limousine
Service is also available at no extra charge.

     —




                              Doc 1  Pg 1  Ln 19     Pos 10
```

1.5 · Close the letter

Now, type the letter's closing.

TYPE **Warmest regards,**

⏎ Press 4 times to return the cursor to the next line and add three blank lines.

TYPE **Ranger David Harris**

⏎ Return the cursor to the next line.

TYPE **Park Reservations**

⏎ Press 3 times to return the cursor to the next line and add two blank lines.

F8 Turn on underlining.

TYPE **See enclosure**

[F8] Turn off underlining.

```
        Frank D. Edwards
        2345 N. Quail Road
        Birdseye, Utah 84666

        Dear Mr. Edwards,

            This letter is a confirmation of your request for a
        traditional log cabin.

            The Mary Todd Lincoln Cabin has been reserved in your name
        for the week of June 10-17, 1984.  The cabin includes three
        bedrooms, a full kitchen, large parlor, and a hot tub.  Limousine
        Service is also available at no extra charge.

        Warmest regards,


        Ranger David Harris
        Park Reservations


        See enclosure
```

Doc 1   Pg 1   Ln 27   Pos 23

1.6   Print and save

Before you print and save the letter you have created, be sure that you have installed your printer according to the installation instructions in the WordPerfect manual. If you are in a classroom, and your computer is not connected to a printer, consult your instructor for directions on how to proceed.

[Shift] [F7] , [1]   Select the *Full Text* option on the Print menu. The letter begins to print.

Remember to release the Shift and F7 keys before typing the "1".

If your printer is set for hand-fed forms, you must press "Go" from the Printer Control menu.

[F7] , [Y]   Begin saving the document.

ENTER   **cabin** as the filename.

A question asks if you want to exit WordPerfect. The question has a *no* already on the screen. Pressing the Enter key confirms that answer.

 Clear the screen without exiting WordPerfect.

Lesson 2

Editing

In this lesson, you create a new paragraph, insert the current date, and make other editing changes to the reservation letter typed in Lesson 1. When you finish, you print the letter, replace the letter on disk with the edited version on your screen, then clear the screen.

While working through the lesson, you learn the following facts about WordPerfect's features:

- Center Page Top to Bottom centers a page at the printer.

- Date inserts the current date.

- Delete EOL (End of Line) erases an entire line of text.

- Delete Word deletes the word at the cursor.

- Flush Right lets you enter text from the right margin.

- Justification needs to be off to print a ragged right margin.

- Retrieve displays a *copy* of the disk file on your screen.

- Reveal Codes lets you see the codes in your document.

- Save (also the Exit key) lets you replace a file on disk with the document on your screen.

- Word Right and Word Left move the cursor one word at a time.

The skills you learn in this lesson can be used to

- Insert text.
- Delete words.
- Delete lines of text.
- Make new paragraphs.

2.1 Retrieve a document

You should have already completed Lesson 1 before starting this lesson. If not, turn to Lesson 1 and complete the steps before continuing.

 Select the Retrieve feature.

ENTER **cabin** as the filename. The letter you created in Lesson 1 appears on the screen.

*Remember to press the Enter key after typing the word **cabin**.*

```
                        Lone Pine National Park
    _
    RESERVATION CONFIRMATION

    Frank D. Edwards
    2345 N. Quail Road
    Birdseye, Utah 84666

    Dear Mr. Edwards,

        This letter is a confirmation of your request for a
    traditional log cabin.

        The Mary Todd Lincoln Cabin has been reserved in your name
    for the week of June 10-17, 1984.  The cabin includes three
    bedrooms, a full kitchen, large parlor, and a hot tub.  Limousine
    Service is also available at no extra charge.

    Warmest regards,



    Ranger David Harris
    Park Reservations


    B:\CABIN                           Doc 1  Pg 1  Ln 1      Pos 10
```

2.2 | Delete text and insert date

Begin editing the letter by deleting a line of text and inserting the current date.

↓ Press 2 times to move to the first letter of "RESERVATION."

Ctrl End Delete the entire line.

Alt F6 Select the Flush Right feature, and the cursor jumps to the right margin.

Shift F5 , **1**   Select the *Insert Text* option on the Date menu to insert the current date.

The date will read "January 1, 1980" if you did not enter the date when you booted your machine.

```
                        Lone Pine National Park

                                              October 3, 1984_

         Frank D. Edwards
         2345 N. Quail Road
         Birdseye, Utah 84666

         Dear Mr. Edwards,

               This letter is a confirmation of your request for a
         traditional log cabin.

               The Mary Todd Lincoln Cabin has been reserved in your name
         for the week of June 10-17, 1984.  The cabin includes three
         bedrooms, a full kitchen, large parlor, and a hot tub.  Limousine
         Service is also available at no extra charge.

         Warmest regards,



         Ranger David Harris
         Park Reservations



         B:\CABIN                              Doc 1  Pg 1  Ln 3      Pos 75
```

2.3   Editing

Now, create and edit a new paragraph.

MOVE   To the "L" in "Limousine."

Back-space   Press 2 times to delete two spaces.

↵   Press 2 times to return the cursor to the next line and add a blank line.

Tab   Insert a tab, and the cursor moves to the next tab stop.

Ctrl →   Press 3 times to move to the word "also."

Ctrl Back-space   Delete the word "also."

Ctrl ←   Move one word to the left.

TYPE   **from the airport to your cabin**

Space Bar	Add a space.
↓	Rewrite the screen.

```
                    Lone Pine National Park

                                         October 3, 1984

       Frank D. Edwards
       2345 N. Quail Road
       Birdseye, Utah 84666

       Dear Mr. Edwards,

           This letter is a confirmation of your request for a
       traditional log cabin.

           The Mary Todd Lincoln Cabin has been reserved in your name
       for the week of June 10-17, 1984.  The cabin includes three
       bedrooms, a full kitchen, large parlor, and a hot tub.

           Limousine Service from the airport to your cabin is
       available at no extra charge._

       Warmest regards,



       B:\CABIN                          Doc 1  Pg 1  Ln 19    Pos 39
```

2.4   Center Page and Right Justification

Both the Center Page and Right Justification features adjust the way the text of your document will appear on the *printed* page.

Home, **Home**, **↑**   Move to the beginning of the document.

Alt F8, **3**   Select the *Center Page* option on the Page Format menu. This centers text vertically on the page. However, the text is centered at the printer— not on the screen.

↵   Exit the Page Format menu.

Ctrl F8, **3**   Select the *Turn off Justification* option on the Print Format menu. Now, the right margin will be uneven when the letter is printed.

⏎ Exit the Print Format menu.

[Alt] [F3] Find the [Center Pg] and [Rt Just Off] codes in the Reveal Codes screen.

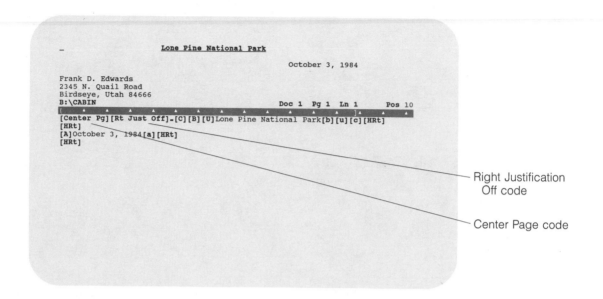

Right Justification
Off code

Center Page code

⏎ Exit the Reveal Codes screen.

2.5 Print and save

Print and save the letter, then clear the screen.

[Shift] [F7] , [1] Select the *Full Text* option on the Print menu. The letter begins to print.

[F7] , [Y] Begin saving the letter.

⏎ , Y Replace the original letter on disk with the edited letter on your screen.

⏎ Clear the screen.

Lesson 3

Formatting

In this lesson, you make several formatting changes to the reservation letter edited in Lesson 2. Some of the changes appear on your screen (margins, double spacing). Some of the changes appear only when the letter is printed (pitch, page length, lines per inch).

You are also introduced to the List Files screen. The List Files screen displays all or part of the files in a drive or directory.

Lesson 12 gives you more practice with the List Files feature.

While working through the lesson, you learn the following facts about WordPerfect's features:

- List Files displays an alphabetical list of the files on a disk.
- List Files lets you retrieve, delete, and print a file.
- Line Format lets you change margins, tabs, and spacing.
- Print Format lets you change pitch and lines per inch.
- Page Format lets you change page length and center the page at the printer.

The skills you learn in this lesson can be used to change the appearance of a printed page.

3.1   Retrieve a document

You should have already completed Lessons 1 and 2 before starting this lesson. If not, turn to those lessons and complete the steps before continuing.

 Select the List Files feature and display all the files on your Learning diskette (or in your default directory). The cursor in the List Files screen is represented by a large reverse video bar that highlights the file (or directory) it rests on.

MOVE To the CABIN filename in the listing.

1 Select the *Retrieve* option to retrieve the cabin letter.

```
                    -
                        Lone Pine National Park
                                          October 3, 1984

          Frank D. Edwards
          2345 N. Quail Road
          Birdseye, Utah 84666

          Dear Mr. Edwards,

               This letter is a confirmation of your request for a
          traditional log cabin.

               The Mary Todd Lincoln Cabin has been reserved in your name
          for the week of June 10-17, 1984.  The cabin includes three
          bedrooms, a full kitchen, large parlor, and a hot tub.

               Limousine Service from the airport to your cabin is
          available at no extra charge.

          Warmest regards,



          B:\CABIN                          Doc 1  Pg 1  Ln 1      Pos 10
```

3.2 Pitch, tab stops, and margins

Begin to reformat by changing the pitch, tab stop settings, and margins.

Ctrl F8 , 1 Select the *Pitch/Font* option on the Print Format menu.

ENTER **12** to change from 10 to 12 pitch.

↵ Keep the same font.

↵ Exit the Print Format menu.

Now that you are printing 12 characters per inch (pitch) instead of 10, your margins need to be wider, and you need to change the tab stop settings.

Shift F8 , 3 Select the *Margins* option on the Line Format menu.

ENTER **12** for the new left margin and **89** for the new right margin.

These settings give you one-inch margins on the left and right sides of your text in 12 pitch.

Shift F8 , 1 Select the *Tabs* option on the Line Format menu.

Ctrl End Erase the current tab stop settings (beginning at position 10) using the Delete EOL feature.

ENTER **12,5** to insert left-justified tabs every 5 spaces beginning at position 12 (the new left margin).

F7 Exit the Tab menu.

```
                      Lone Pine National Park
      _
                                                October 3, 1984

      Frank D. Edwards
      2345 N. Quail Road
      Birdseye, Utah 84666

      Dear Mr. Edwards,

           This letter is a confirmation of your request for a traditional log
      cabin.

           The Mary Todd Lincoln Cabin has been reserved in your name for the week
      of June 10-17, 1984.  The cabin includes three bedrooms, a full kitchen, large
      parlor, and a hot tub.

           Limousine Service from the airport to your cabin is available at no extra
      charge.

      Warmest regards,




      B:\CABIN                                Doc 1   Pg 1   Ln 1        Pos 12
```

3.3 Lines per inch and text lines

Now, change the lines per inch (number of lines that will be printed per each inch) and the text lines (the lines you will actually use for text on a printed page) in the document.

Ctrl F8 , 2 Select the *Lines per Inch* option on the Print Format menu.

ENTER **8** to change from 6 to 8 lines per inch.

↵ Exit the Print Format menu.

Now that you have increased the number of lines per inch that are printed, you can increase the number of text lines on the page.

Alt F8 , 4 Select the *Page Length* option on the Page Format menu. The Page Length menu appears.

3 Select *Other* from the menu. This lets you create your own settings.

↵ Leave the form length (actual length, in lines, of the paper you are using) at 66 lines.

ENTER **72** to change the text lines from 54 to 72.

To arrive at 72 text lines on 11-inch paper, subtract one inch from the top and bottom for the margins. This leaves 9 inches for text, multiplied by 8 lines per inch equals 72.

Notice that the form length stays the same while the number of text lines increases. Form length is *always* 6 lines per inch; the Lines per Inch feature only affects the text lines on a page.

⏎   Exit the Page Format menu.

Alt F3   Find the [LPI:8] and [Pg Lnth:66,72] codes in the Reveal Codes screen.

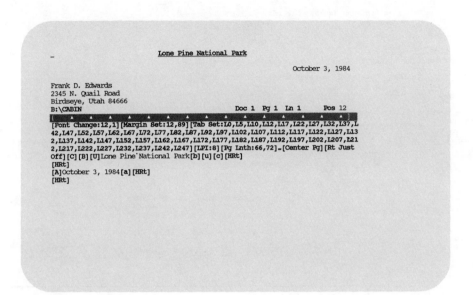

3.4   Double spacing

While you are in the Reveal Codes screen, you can use the Search feature.

F2 , Tab   Select the Search feature and insert a Tab code as the search string.

F2   Begin the search. The cursor stops to the right of the first Tab code in the letter.

←   Move to the left of the Tab code.

⏎   Exit the Reveal Codes screen.

| `Shift` `F8` , `4` | Select the *Spacing* option on the Line Format menu. |
| ENTER | **2** for double spacing. |

```
     Dear Mr. Edwards,

     _     This letter is a confirmation of your request for a traditional log
     cabin.


          The Mary Todd Lincoln Cabin has been reserved in your name for the week
     of June 10-17, 1984.  The cabin includes three bedrooms, a full kitchen, large
     parlor, and a hot tub.


          Limousine Service from the airport to your cabin is available at no extra
     charge.


     Warmest regards,

     B:\CABIN                                 Doc 1  Pg 1  Ln 11      Pos 12
```

3.5 Save and print

Save the letter using a new filename, clear the screen, then print the letter.

`F7` , `Y`	Begin saving the letter.
ENTER	**cabin.1** as the filename.
`↵`	Clear the screen.
`F5` , `↵`	Select the List Files feature and display all the files on your Learning diskette (or in your default directory).
TYPE	**cabin.1** to highlight the CABIN.1 file using the Name Search feature.

⏎ End the name search.

4 Select the *Print* option and print the CABIN.1 file. If this letter does not print correctly, your printer may not be able to print in 12 pitch.

Lone Pine National Park

Frank D. Edwards
2345 N. Quail Road
Birdseye, Utah 84666   October 3, 1984

Dear Mr. Edwards,

This letter is a confirmation of your request for a traditional log cabin.

The Mary Todd Lincoln Cabin has been reserved in your name for the week of June 10-17, 1984. The cabin includes three bedrooms, a full kitchen, large parlor, and a hot tub.

Limousine Service from the airport to your cabin is available at no extra charge.

Warmest regards,

Ranger David Harris
Park Reservations

See enclosure

3.6	**Delete a file**

To complete the lesson, delete the first revision of your letter which is still saved under the filename CABIN.

TYPE **cabin** to highlight the CABIN file using the Name Search feature.

⏎ End the name search.

You may only need to type the first letter or two of the name.

2 , Y   Select the *Delete* option and delete the CABIN file. If you are doing Lessons 1, 2, and 3 again, you may also want to delete the CABIN.1 file at this point.

F7   Exit the List Files screen.

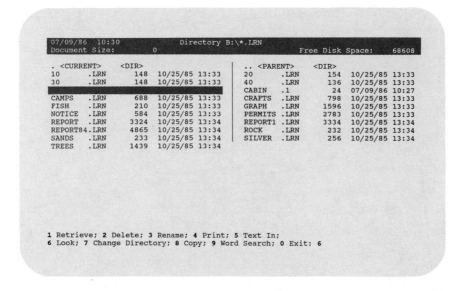

```
07/09/86  10:30                Directory B:\*.LRN
Document Size:          0                       Free Disk Space:      68608

.  <CURRENT>       <DIR>                    ..  <PARENT>       <DIR>
10       .LRN         148   10/25/85 13:33   20       .LRN         154   10/25/85 13:33
30       .LRN         148   10/25/85 13:33   40       .LRN         136   10/25/85 13:33
                                             CABIN    .1            24   07/09/86 10:27
CAMPS    .LRN         688   10/25/85 13:33   CRAFTS   .LRN         798   10/25/85 13:33
FISH     .LRN         210   10/25/85 13:33   GRAPH    .LRN        1596   10/25/85 13:33
NOTICE   .LRN         584   10/25/85 13:33   PERMITS  .LRN        2783   10/25/85 13:33
REPORT   .LRN        3324   10/25/85 13:34   REPORT1  .LRN        3334   10/25/85 13:34
REPORT84 .LRN        4865   10/25/85 13:34   ROCK     .LRN         232   10/25/85 13:34
SANDS    .LRN         233   10/25/85 13:34   SILVER   .LRN         256   10/25/85 13:34
TREES    .LRN        1439   10/25/85 13:34



1 Retrieve; 2 Delete; 3 Rename; 4 Print; 5 Text In;
6 Look; 7 Change Directory; 8 Copy; 9 Word Search; 0 Exit: 6
```

Troubleshooting

Every time you press a key, you send a message to WordPerfect. Sometimes the message tells WordPerfect to display a character on the screen.

Whenever you press a WordPerfect key to change a setting (margins, tabs) or perform a task (center, bold, underline), a code is placed in your text. These codes are enclosed in brackets [ ] and are only seen in the Reveal Codes screen.

In this lesson, you have a chance to correct several common problems, including extra text, extra codes, and *hidden* text. You also learn to reset the format to its initial settings by deleting format codes.

While working through the lesson, you learn the following facts about WordPerfect's features:

- Block and Delete let you delete a block of text.

- The cursor keys let you move the cursor in the Reveal Codes screen.

- Backspace and Delete delete codes and text in the Reveal Codes screen.

- Search lets you search for tab, spacing, and other codes in the Reveal Codes screen.

- Initial settings of WordPerfect can be set again by deleting intervening format codes.

- The Center code can hide text on the screen.

The skills you learn in this lesson can be used to

- Detect unwanted text.
- Search and delete unwanted codes.
- Check a document with the Reveal Codes screen.
- Solve some printing problems.

4.1 Retrieve and print a document

By retrieving and printing the Buffalo Permits document, you will be able to see some of the errors you need to correct.

 Select the Retrieve feature.

ENTER **permits.lrn** as the filename.

 Select the *Page* option on the Print menu to print only the first page of the document.

Now, find and circle the errors as in the following illustration:

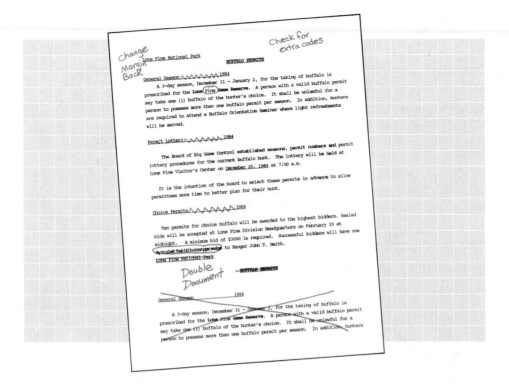

4.2 Block delete

Begin correcting by deleting a duplicate copy of the permit document.

MOVE To the end of the first copy of the document (Line 50 Position 65).

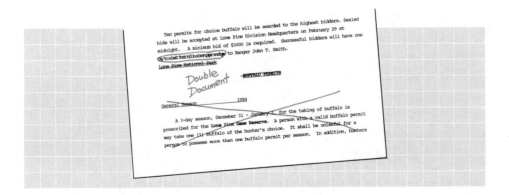

Notice that a duplicate copy of the document is in the file. Often, when the screen is clear, you may think a document is gone and retrieve it again. However, the document may be just off the screen. You now have two documents (one off and one on the screen). When you save the document on your screen, both documents are placed in the file on disk.

| Alt | F4 | Turn on Block.

| Home |, | Home |, | ↓ | Move to the end of the second copy.

| Back-space |, | Y | Delete the duplicate copy of the document.

| Home |, | Home |, | ↑ | Return to the beginning of the first copy.

4.3 Adjust format settings

In this section, you change several formats back to their initial settings by deleting some intervening codes. As you delete codes, watch for any noticeable effects on the document.

| Alt | F3 | Display the Reveal Codes screen.

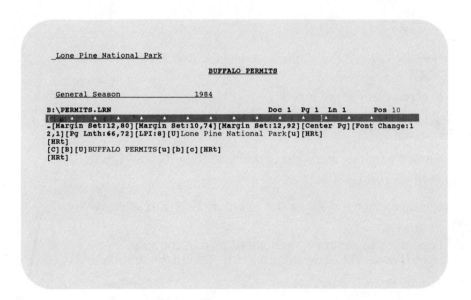

Notice that there are three margin sets at the beginning of the document. To change the margin setting from 12 and 92 (the only margin set WordPerfect is using) to the initial setting of 10 and 74, all three margin sets should be deleted.

| Del | Press 3 times to delete the three margin settings.

| → | Move to the right of the Center Page code.

[Del] Press 3 times to delete the Font Change, Page Length, and Lines per Inch codes. Once these codes are deleted, WordPerfect uses the initial settings of 10 pitch, 66 form length, 54 text lines, and 6 lines per inch.

```
Lone Pine National Park

                         BUFFALO PERMITS

General Season                        1984

B:\PERMITS.LRN                              Doc 1  Pg 1  Ln 1      Pos 10
[                                                           ]
[Center Pg]_[U]Lone Pine National Park[u][HRt]
[HRt]
[C][B][U]BUFFALO PERMITS[u][b][c][HRt]
[HRt]
```

Now that you have deleted the 12 pitch code, you also need to delete the tab setting.

[F2] Select the ▶Search feature.

[Shift] [F8], [1] Select the *Tabs* option on the Line Format menu to insert a [Tab Set] code as the search string.

[F2] Begin the search. The cursor stops just to the right of the [Tab Set] code.

[Back-space] Delete the [Tab Set] code.

The tab stops now change back to the initial setting of one every 5 positions.

Tabs have been used to separate each subtitle from the year. Notice the [Undrl Style:7] code. This style underlines the Tabs in the subtitles.

[Del] Delete the [Undrl Style:7] code.

The style now changes back to the initial setting of non-continuous. Notice that the tabs are not underlined in the top half of the screen.

⏎ Return to the normal screen and notice the changes in format.

```
                        BUFFALO PERMITS

General Season                1984
       A 3-day season, December 31 - January 2, for the taking of

buffalo is prescribed for the Lone Pine Game Reserve.  A person

with a valid buffalo permit may take one (1) buffalo of the

hunter's choice.  It shall be unlawful for a person to possess

more than one buffalo permit per season.  In addition, hunters

are required to attend a Buffalo Orientation Seminar where light

refreshments will be served.


Permit Lottery                1984



B:\PERMITS.LRN                            Doc 1  Pg 1  Ln 5       Pos 10
```

Next, you change the spacing in the document back to the initial setting of single spacing by deleting the double spacing code.

F2 Select the ▶Search feature.

Shift F8 , 4 Select the *Spacing* option on the Line Format menu to insert a [Spacing Set] code as the search string.

[F2] Begin the search. The cursor stops just to the right of the [Spacing Set] code.

[Back-space] , [Y] Delete the [Spacing Set] code.

```
       Lone Pine National Park

                      BUFFALO PERMITS

       General Season              1984      .

       _    A 3-day season, December 31 - January 2, for the taking of
       buffalo is prescribed for the Lone Pine Game Reserve.  A person
       with a valid buffalo permit may take one (1) buffalo of the
       hunter's choice.  It shall be unlawful for a person to possess
       more than one buffalo permit per season.  In addition, hunters
       are required to attend a Buffalo Orientation Seminar where light
       refreshments will be served.

       Permit Lottery               1984

            The Board of Big Game Control established seasons, permit
       numbers and permit lottery procedures for the current buffalo
       hunt.  The lottery will be held at Lone Pine Visitor's Center on
       December 25, 1984 at 7:00 a.m.

            It is the intention of the board to select these permits in
       advance to allow permittees more time to better plan for their

       B:\PERMITS.LRN                           Doc 1  Pg 1  Ln 8     Pos 10
```

4.4 Correct the bolding problem

Notice that the word "Pine" is not bolded in the first paragraph.

[F2] Select the ▶Search feature.

[F6] Select the Bold feature to insert a [Bold] code as the search string.

[F2] Begin the search. The cursor stops just to the right of the first Bold code.

[Alt] [F3] Display the Reveal Codes screen and notice that "Lone" and "Game Reserve" are bolded separately.

[↵] Exit the Reveal Codes screen.

[Alt] [F4] Turn on Block.

TYPE ve to highlight the phrase.

[F6] Bold the phrase.

[Alt] [F3] Display the Reveal Codes screen and notice that there is only one set of bold codes now.

[↵] Exit the Reveal Codes screen.

Hidden text

The last line on the printed page has extra text printed on top of the existing text. This extra text does not appear on the screen because it is *hidden* by a misplaced Center code.

Home , Home , ↓   Move to the end of the document.

Alt F3   Display the Reveal Codes screen. Notice that the phrase "a brown paper envelope" appears in front of the [C] code in the Reveal Codes screen, but does not appear on the normal screen.

Back-space   Delete the Center codes.

The phrase hidden by the Center code now appears in the document.

↵   Exit the Reveal Codes screen.

```
Division Headquarters on February 29 at midnight.   A minimum bid
of $3000 is required.   Successful bidders will have one day to
submit their bid in a brown paper envelope to Ranger John T.
Smith. _




B:\PERMITS.LRN                              Doc 1  Pg 1  Ln 34     Pos 18
```

Print and save

Print and save the edited letter, then clear the screen.

Shift F7 , 2   Select the *Page* option on the Print menu. The document begins to print; it is only one page long.

F7 , Y   Begin saving the document.

ENTER **permits.1** as the filename.

 Clear the screen.

Lone Pine National Park   **BUFFALO PERMITS**

1984

General Season
    A 3-day season, December 31 - January 2, for the taking of
buffalo is prescribed for the **Lone Pine Game Reserve.** A person
with a valid buffalo permit may take one (1) buffalo of the
hunter's choice. It shall be unlawful for a person to possess
more than one buffalo permit per season. In addition, hunters
are required to attend a Buffalo Orientation Seminar where light
refreshments will be served.

1984

Permit Lottery
    The Board of Big Game Control established seasons, permit
numbers and permit lottery procedures for the current buffalo
hunt.   The lottery will be held at Lone Pine Visitor's Center on
December 25, 1984 at 7:00 a.m.

    It is the intention of the board to select these permits in
advance to allow permittees more time to better plan for their
hunt.

1984

Choice Permits
.   Ten permits for choice buffalo will be awarded to the
highest bidders. Sealed bids will be accepted at Lone Pine
Division Headquarters on February 29 at midnight.   A minimum bid
of $3000 is required. Successful bidders will have one day to
submit their bid in a brown paper envelope to Ranger John T.
Smith.

Moving Text

After typing the first draft of a document, much of the editing you do deals with rearranging your thoughts into an order that makes sense.

In this lesson, you are introduced to the WordPerfect features that help you rearrange and edit a sentence, paragraph, or any block of text. You also learn to create a *hanging* paragraph, and to use the Escape key to repeat a character.

While working through the lesson, you learn the following facts about WordPerfect's features:

- Block and Switch help you change a title to uppercase letters.
- Center can center an existing line of text.
- Move helps you move a sentence, paragraph, or block of text.
- ◀Margin Release and Indent can help you create a hanging paragraph.
- Escape can help you repeat a character.
- Block can highlight a block of text to be printed.

The skills you learn in this lesson can be used to

- Rearrange your text.
- Center, bold, and underline existing text.
- Save text in a temporary file while in WordPerfect.
- Create a line of characters using the Escape key.
- Print part of a page.

5.1 Retrieve a document

Retrieve the Tree Permit document for editing.

 `Shift` `F10` Select the Retrieve feature.

ENTER **trees.lrn** as the filename.

```
Lone Pine National Park
                      Christmas Tree Harvest - 1984
        There are several varieties of evergreen trees which can be
   harvested.  They are not hard to tell apart as the leaves
   (needles) and cones are usually quite different:

        2.   Pines - Needles gathered together at the base
             in bunches of one to five in a little sheath
             that often wears off after the first year.

        3.   Spruces - Needles scattered over the twigs
             singly, less than an inch long.  Cones have
             thick woody scales.

        1.   Juniper or Cedar - Needles reduced to little
             green scales on the twigs, cones reduced to
             small bluish berries.

        It is essential that anyone cutting Christmas trees for
   personal or commercial use be able to identify the trees that can
   be legally harvested.


   B:\TREES.LRN                          Doc 1  Pg 1  Ln 1      Pos 10
```

5.2 Center, capitalize, and underline

The heading of this document needs to be centered, capitalized, and underlined.

[Shift][F6] Turn on centering.

[Alt][F4] Turn on Block.

[Home], [→] Highlight the title.

`Shift` `F3` , `1`   Select the *Uppercase* option on the Switch menu to change the title to uppercase letters.

`F8`   Underline the title.

```
              LONE PINE NATIONAL PARK

           Christmas Tree Harvest - 1984

        There are several varieties of evergreen trees which can be
   harvested.  They are not hard to tell apart as the leaves
   (needles) and cones are usually quite different:

        2.   Pines - Needles gathered together at the base
             in bunches of one to five in a little sheath
             that often wears off after the first year.

        3.   Spruces - Needles scattered over the twigs
             singly, less than an inch long.  Cones have
             thick woody scales.

        1.   Juniper or Cedar - Needles reduced to little
             green scales on the twigs, cones reduced to
             small bluish berries.

        It is essential that anyone cutting Christmas trees for
   personal or commercial use be able to identify the trees that can
   be legally harvested.


   B:\TREES.LRN                          Doc 1  Pg 1  Ln 1      Pos 54
```

5.3   Move a paragraph

Continue editing this document by moving the fifth paragraph to the beginning of the text.

MOVE   To the left margin at the beginning of the fifth paragraph (Line 21 Position 10).

`Ctrl` `F4` , `2`   Select the *Paragraph* option on the Move menu to highlight the paragraph.

`1`   Cut the paragraph from the screen. It is automatically saved in a temporary file.

MOVE   To the left margin at the beginning of the first paragraph (Line 5 Position 10).

`Ctrl` `F4` , `5` Select the *Retrieve Text* option on the Move menu to retrieve the paragraph.

```
                    LONE PINE NATIONAL PARK

                 Christmas Tree Harvest - 1984

 _      It is essential that anyone cutting Christmas trees for
personal or commercial use be able to identify the trees that can
be legally harvested.

        There are several varieties of evergreen trees which can be
harvested.  They are not hard to tell apart as the leaves
(needles) and cones are usually quite different:

        2.    Pines - Needles gathered together at the base
              in bunches of one to five in a little sheath
              that often wears off after the first year.

        3.    Spruces - Needles scattered over the twigs
              singly, less than an inch long.  Cones have
              thick woody scales.

        1.    Juniper or Cedar - Needles reduced to little
              green scales on the twigs, cones reduced to
              small bluish berries.



B:\TREES.LRN                          Doc 1  Pg 1  Ln 5       Pos 10
```

5.4   Arrange the descriptions

The tree descriptions should be arranged in their correct numeric order.

MOVE To the "J" in "Juniper" (Line 21).

`Home` , `Home` , `Home` , `←` Move the cursor ahead of any codes in the line.

`Alt` `F4` Turn on Block.

MOVE To the left margin at the beginning of the sixth paragraph (Line 25 Position 10).

`Ctrl` `F4` , `1` Select the *Cut Block* option on the Block Move menu to cut the highlighted paragraph.

MOVE To the first line of the third paragraph (Line 13).

`Home` , `Home` , `Home` , `←` Move the cursor ahead of any codes in the line.

`Ctrl` `F4` , `5` Select the *Retrieve Text* option on the Move menu to retrieve the paragraph.

```
                    LONE PINE NATIONAL PARK

                  Christmas Tree Harvest - 1984

          It is essential that anyone cutting Christmas trees for
     personal or commercial use be able to identify the trees that can
     be legally harvested.

          There are several varieties of evergreen trees which can be
     harvested.  They are not hard to tell apart as the leaves
     (needles) and cones are usually quite different:

  _      1.   Juniper or Cedar -  Needles reduced to little
               green scales on the twigs, cones reduced to
               small bluish berries.

         2.   Pines - Needles gathered together at the base
               in bunches of one to five in a little sheath
               that often wears off after the first year.

         3.   Spruces - Needles scattered over the twigs
               singly, less than an inch long.  Cones have
               thick woody scales.


     B:\TREES.LRN                          Doc 1  Pg 1  Ln 13      Pos 10
```

5.5   Create a tree description

Now add another tree description in the form of a *hanging* paragraph.

MOVE To the blank line before the sixth paragraph (Line 24 Position 10).

`↵` Add a blank line.

`Shift` `F4` Press 2 times to indent to the second tab stop from the margin. The ◆Indent◆ feature indents an equal amount from both margins. Use the ◆Indent key if you don't want the paragraph indented from the right margin.

`Shift` `Tab` Select the ◆Margin Release feature to release the first line one tab stop.

A hanging paragraph indents all but the first line of the paragraph.

TYPE **4.** to number the paragraph.

`Tab` Insert a Tab to move to the second tab stop from the margin.

TYPE **<u>Firs</u> - Needles flat and blunt, mostly grooved on upper side, leaving flat round scars when they fall off.**

⏎ Add a blank line.

```
      It is essential that anyone cutting Christmas trees for
personal or commercial use be able to identify the trees that can
be legally harvested.

      There are several varieties of evergreen trees which can be
harvested.  They are not hard to tell apart as the leaves
(needles) and cones are usually quite different:

      1.   Juniper or Cedar - Needles reduced to little
           green scales on the twigs, cones reduced to
           small bluish berries.

      2.   Pines - Needles gathered together at the base
           in bunches of one to five in a little sheath
           that often wears off after the first year.

      3.   Spruces - Needles scattered over the twigs
           singly, less than an inch long.  Cones have
           thick woody scales.

      4.   Firs - Needles flat and blunt, mostly grooved
           on upper side, leaving flat round scars when
           they fall off.
  _


B:\TREES.LRN                          Doc 1  Pg 1  Ln 28     Pos 10
```

5.6   Copy a sentence

Use a sentence from the Spruces tree description in the new Firs description.

MOVE To "Cones" in the Spruces tree description (Line 22 Position 53).

[Ctrl] [F4] , [1] Select the *Sentence* option on the Move menu to highlight the sentence.

[2] Copy the sentence on the screen. It is automatically saved in a temporary file.

MOVE To the end of the Firs tree description (Line 27 Position 34).

[Ctrl] [F4] , [5] Select the *Retrieve Text* option on the Move menu to retrieve the sentence.

Space Bar Press 2 times to add space between the sentences.

← Rewrite the screen.

```
        It is essential that anyone cutting Christmas trees for
personal or commercial use be able to identify the trees that can
be legally harvested.

        There are several varieties of evergreen trees which can be
harvested.  They are not hard to tell apart as the leaves
(needles) and cones are usually quite different:

        1.    Juniper or Cedar -  Needles reduced to little
              green scales on the twigs, cones reduced to
              small bluish berries.

        2.    Pines - Needles gathered together at the base
              in bunches of one to five in a little sheath
              that often wears off after the first year.

        3.    Spruces - Needles scattered over the twigs
              singly, less than an inch long.  Cones have
              thick woody scales.

        4.    Firs - Needles flat and blunt, mostly grooved
              on upper side, leaving flat round scars when
              they fall off. _Cones have thick woody
              scales.

B:\TREES.LRN                              Doc 1  Pg 1  Ln 27    Pos 35
```

5.7 Add another category

You need to add one more category to the request slip at the bottom of the Tree Permit document.

MOVE To "Type of tree" on the request slip (Line 51).

Home , **→** Move to the end of the line.

Tab Press 2 times to add extra space in the line.

TYPE **Number of trees**

Space Bar Press 2 times to add extra space after the text.

F8 Turn on underlining.

Esc , **1** , **2** Change the repetition number from 8 to 12.

Space Bar Create a line 12 spaces long.

F8 Turn off underlining.

```
        scales.
            If you are interested in harvesting trees in 1984, fill out
        the request form below and send it to:

                    John T. Smith
                    Park Director
                    Lone Pine National Park
                    Fremont, Utah  84666

        ------------------------------------------------------------------

                    Request for Tree Harvest

        Name _____          Date of Harvest _____

        Address _____

                _____


        Type of tree _____          Number of trees _____

        B:\TREES.LRN                                 Doc 1  Pg 1  Ln 51      Pos 74
```

5.8 Block print

Now, print only the request slip.

MOVE To the blank line just before the request slip (Line 37).

Alt F4 Turn on Block.

Home , Home , ↓ Highlight the request slip.

Shift F7 , Y Select the Print Block feature to print the request slip.

Alt F4 Turn off Block.

5.9 Print and save

Print and save the edited permit document, then clear the screen.

Shift F7 , 1 Select the *Full Text* option on the Print menu to print the permit.

F7 , Y Begin saving the permit.

ENTER **trees.1** as the filename.

⏎ Clear the screen.

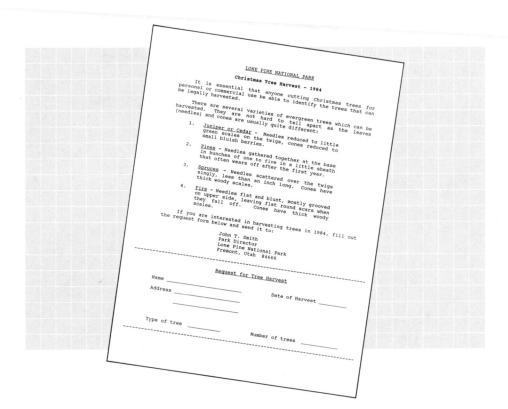

LONE PINE NATIONAL PARK

Christmas Tree Harvest - 1984

It is essential that anyone cutting Christmas trees for personal or commercial use be able to identify the trees that can be legally harvested.

There are several varieties of evergreen trees which can be harvested. They are not hard to tell apart as the leaves (needles) and cones are usually quite different:

1. Juniper or Cedar - Needles reduced to little green scales on the twigs, cones reduced to small bluish berries.

2. Pines - Needles gathered together at the base in bunches of one to five in a little sheath that often wears off after the first year.

3. Spruces - Needles scattered over the twigs singly, less than an inch long. Cones have thick woody scales.

4. Firs - Needles flat and blunt, mostly grooved on upper side, leaving flat round scars when they fall off. Cones have thick woody scales.

If you are interested in harvesting trees in 1984, fill out the request form below and send it to:

John T. Smith
Park Director
Lone Pine National Park
Fremont, Utah 84666

Request for Tree Harvest

Name _____

Address _____   Date of Harvest _____
        _____

Type of tree _____   Number of trees _____

Spell-Checking

The Speller that comes with your WordPerfect package not only checks the spelling of words, but also checks for double words, words with numbers, and lets you do a word count without checking the document.

In this lesson, you use the Speller to check Ranger Douglas R. LaRue's annual report. Each step sets up a situation, then helps you discover another feature of the Speller.

While working through the lesson, you learn the following facts about WordPerfect's Speller:

- Skip ignores a word for the rest of the document.

- The Speller lists alternate spellings for each word not found in the dictionary list.

- Delete 2nd automatically deletes the second word of a double word.

- Words with Numbers can be disabled while spell-checking.

- Look Up lets you see the words in the speller that match a word pattern.

- Edit lets you move into the document to edit a word.

  The skills you learn in this lesson can be used to

- Spell-check a word, page, or document before it is printed.
- Check for words with numbers.
- Look up words that match a pattern.

6.1 Retrieve a document

Retrieve the Annual Report document. This is the document you will be spell-checking.

 Select the Retrieve feature.

ENTER **report.lrn** as the filename.

```
                        Lone Pine National Park
                             Annual Report
                                 1984




                               Compiled by
                         Ranger Douglas R. LaRue
                              Park Director
==============================================================================
                                PREFACE


           This report is a summary of the year's activities,

        as well as goals for the four devisions of Lone Pine

        National Park for 1985.


B:\REPORT.LRN                               Doc 1  Pg 1  Ln 1      Pos 10
```

6.2   Start the Speller

After retrieving the annual report, you want to spell-check the entire document.

REPLACE   Your Learning diskette in drive B with your Speller diskette.

[Ctrl] [F2]   Select the Spell feature and the Check menu appears.

If you are running WordPerfect from a hard disk, make sure that LEX.WP is in your WordPerfect directory.

```
                        Lone Pine National Park
                             Annual Report
                                 1984




                               Compiled by
                         Ranger Douglas R. LaRue
                              Park Director
==============================================================================
                                PREFACE


           This report is a summary of the year's activities,

        as well as goals for the four devisions of Lone Pine

        National Park for 1985.


Check: 1 Word; 2 Page; 3 Document; 4 Change Dictionary; 5 Look Up; 6 Count
```

[3]   Begin spell-checking the entire document.

6.3   Skip a word

```
                    Compiled by
             Ranger Douglas R.  LaRue
                   Park Director
=======================================================================
                      PREFACE


=======================================================================

      A. large          B. lair           C. larry
      D. laugher        E. lawyer         F. layer
      G. leer           H. leery          I. liar
      J. lira           K. lire           L. lore
      M. lorry          N. lower          O. lowery
      P. lure           Q. lyra           R. lyre




Not Found!  Select Word or Menu Option (0=Continue): 0
1 Skip Once; 2 Skip; 3 Add Word; 4 Edit; 5 Look Up
```

The Speller stops at the name "LaRue." You want to skip the name and continue spell-checking.

2   Skip the word for the rest of the document.

6.4   Automatically correct a word

The Speller stops at the word "devisions." The correct spelling is displayed in the list.

```
        This report is a summary of the year's activities,
     as well as goals for the four devisions of Lone Pine
     National Park for 1985.


     Division I - Big Game Reserve
     =============================================================================

     A. decisions          B. divisions          C. divisionis
     D. divisions




Not Found!  Select Word or Menu Option (0=Continue): 0
1 Skip Once; 2 Skip; 3 Add Word; 4 Edit; 5 Look Up
```

B Insert the correct spelling of the word.

6.5 Delete a double word

```
Permits
        During the 1984 Hunting season the Lone Pine Game
Game Reserve offered permits for the taking of Deer,
Elk, Antelope, Moose, Buffalo, Rocky Mountain Goat, and
Bighorn Sheep.  The permits were issued by lottery, bid,
and once-in-a-lifetime priorities.  The hunting hours




Double Word!   1 2 Skip; 3 Delete 2nd; 4 Edit; 5 Disable double work checking_
```

The Speller stops at a double occurrence of the word "Game." You want to delete the second word.

3 Delete the second "Game" and continue spell-checking.

6.6 Ignore words with numbers

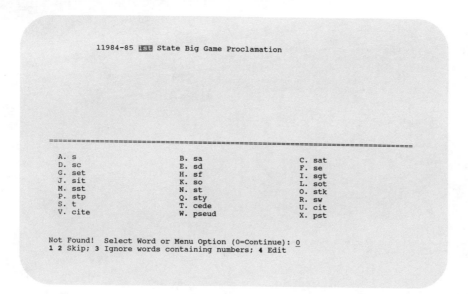

The Speller checks a footnote and finds a word with a number. You want the Speller to skip all words in the document that contain numbers.

3 Ignore all words with numbers in the document.

Look up a word

```
   4.   The Blue Card does not need to be on the person of
        the hunter while in the field;  it need only be
        presented when receiving the game permit.

   5.   Any violation of the regulation will mean automatic
        forefieture of the Blue Card (except in "Doner
        Heights").

        The goals and improvements for the 1985-86 hunts


========================================================================

   A. forefather




Not Found!  Select Word or Menu Option (0=Continue): 0
1 Skip Once; 2 Skip; 3 Add Word; 4 Edit; 5 Look Up
```

The Speller stops at the word "forefieture" but does not display the correct spelling on the screen.

[5] Select the *Look Up* option and the "Word Pattern:" message appears.

ENTER **f*f*ture**

All the words that begin with "f," have one or more characters followed by another "f," have one or more characters, and end with "ture" are listed on the screen.

[A] Insert the correct spelling into your document.

Manually correct a word

```
    4.    The Blue Card does not need to be on the person of
          the hunter while in the field;  it need only be
          presented when receiving the game permit.

    5.    Any violation of the regulation will mean automatic
          forfeiture of the Blue Card (except in "Doner
          Heights").

          The goals and improvements for the 1985-86 hunts

==============================================================================
    A. diner            B. doer             C. done
    D. donee            E. donor            F. doper
    G. doser            H. doter            I. dover
    J. dower            K. downer           L. dozer
    M. denier           N. diener           O. dinar
    P. diner            Q. dinner           R. donor
    S. downer           T. downier


Not Found!  Select Word or Menu Option (0=Continue): 0
1 Skip Once; 2 Skip; 3 Add Word; 4 Edit; 5 Look Up
```

The Speller stops at the name "Doner." You need to correct the spelling but do not want to add the name to the dictionary.

4 | Move the cursor into the document.

→ | Press 2 times to move to "n".

TYPE **n**

↵ | Exit the document and return to the Speller screen.

2 | Skip the corrected spelling for the rest of the document.

Phonetically correct a word

```
        was able to meet most of its outstanding obligations.

        The program improvement proposal for the 1985-86 year

        can, in part, be funded  thru  park revenues.  However,

        the donated funds mentioned in the proposal are needed

        to complete the 1985-86 projects.



=========================================================================
        A. thou              B. thrum             C. thur
      . D. three             E. threw             F. throe
        G. through           H. throughway        I. throw
        J. throwaway         K. thruway




    Not Found!  Select Word or Menu Option (0=Continue): 0
    1 Skip Once; 2 Skip; 3 Add Word; 4 Edit; 5 Look Up
```

The Speller stops at the word "thru." The correct spelling is displayed because of WordPerfect's built-in phonetic search.

G Insert the correct spelling of the word.

6.10 Exit the Speller

```
        Because of increased revenues during 1984, the park
    was able to meet most of its outstanding obligations.
    The program improvement proposal for the 1985-86 year
    can, in part, be funded through park revenues.  However,
    the donated funds mentioned in the proposal are needed
    to complete the 1985-86 projects.




    Word Count: 460                 Press any key to continue_
```

Spell-checking is over and you see a Word Count at the bottom of the screen.

⏎ Exit the Speller.

If you are using two disk drives, replace the Speller diskette with the Learning diskette before continuing.

F7 , N , ⏎ Clear the screen.

Lesson 7

Footnotes/Page Numbers

Whether you are writing a term paper for a college class or compiling a major investment proposal, WordPerfect provides features that help you create a pleasant format to quickly document your research.

In this lesson, you add a quote and footnote to the Lone Pine Annual Report, number pages with a header, and edit using a split screen and the Replace feature.

While working through the lesson, you learn the following facts about WordPerfect's features:

- Center Page Top to Bottom lets you print a page of text that is centered vertically.

- Spacing and Indent help you format a quote on the page.

- Footnotes are numbered automatically for you.

- Window lets you display two documents on your screen at the same time.

- The Tab Ruler can be placed anywhere to split the screen.

- Replace helps you quickly change characters in your document.

- Search can help you move through your document.

- New Page Number lets you start page numbering with any number and on any page.

- Page numbering can be done in a header.

The skills you learn in this lesson can be used to

- Create reports and term papers for school.
- Document your research with footnotes.
- Edit two documents at the same time.
- Create advanced papers such as proposals, theses, and dissertations.

7.1 Retrieve a document

Retrieve the Annual Report and center the title page.

 Select the Retrieve feature.

ENTER **report1.lrn** as the filename.

`Alt` `F8` , `3` Select the *Center Page Top to Bottom* option on the Page Format menu to center the text vertically on the title page. The text will not be centered on the page until you print the report.

`↵` Exit the Page Format menu.

```
                    Lone Pine National Park
                        Annual Report
                           1984




                        Compiled by
                  Ranger Douglas R. LaRue
                       Park Director
=================================================================================
                          PREFACE


         This report is a summary of the year's activities,

      as well as goals for the four devisions of Lone Pine

      National Park for 1985.


B:\REPORT84.LRN                         Doc 1  Pg 1  Ln 1      Pos 10
```

Change spacing and indent

You will be inserting a quotation into the report, so change to single spacing and indent to prepare for the quoted material.

`PgDn` Press 2 times to move to the top of page 3.

`Esc` , `1` , `2` , `↓` Move to Line 25 Position 15.

`Shift` `F8` , `4` Select the *Spacing* option on the Line Format menu to change the line spacing.

ENTER **1** to begin single spacing.

<kbd>Shift</kbd> <kbd>F4</kbd> Select the ▶Indent◀ feature to begin indenting one tab stop from the left and right margins for the quotation.

<kbd>Tab</kbd> Insert a Tab to indent the first line of the quotation an extra tab stop.

```
                    Big Game Reserve


    Permits
                During the 1984 Hunting season the Lone Pine Game

            Reserve offered permits for the taking of Deer, Elk,

            Antelope, Moose, Buffalo, Rocky Mountain Goat, and

            Bighorn Sheep.  The permits were issued by lottery, bid,

            and once-in-a-lifetime priorities.  The hunting hours

            were continued as per recommendation of the 1983 program

            improvement proposal (ANPI-83-LPNP):
                            HUNTING HOURS

                All permits were monitored by the Ranger and
    B:\REPORT1.LRN                         Doc 1  Pg 3  Ln 25      Pos 25
```

7.3 Type the quotation

Now type the quotation at this spot, then change back to double spacing.

TYPE **It is unlawful to take big game except during daylight hours. Daylight hours are defined as that period between one-half hour before official sunrise to one-half hour after official sunset.**

<kbd>↵</kbd> End indenting and return the cursor to the next line.

Shift F8 , 4   Select the *Spacing* option on the Line Format menu to change the line spacing.

ENTER   **2** to begin double spacing again.

```
Permits
            During the 1984 Hunting season the Lone Pine Game

        Reserve offered permits for the taking of Deer, Elk,

        Antelope, Moose, Buffalo, Rocky Mountain Goat, and

        Bighorn Sheep.  The permits were issued by lottery, bid,

        and once-in-a-lifetime priorities.  The hunting hours

        were continued as per recommendation of the 1983 program

        improvement proposal (ANPI-83-LPNP):
                              HUNTING HOURS
                It is unlawful to take big game except
            during daylight hours.  Daylight hours are
            defined as that period between one-half hour
            before official sunrise to one-half hour after
            official sunset.
            _

        B:\REPORT1.LRN                         Doc 1  Pg 3  Ln 30    Pos 15
```

7.4   Create a footnote

You need to create a footnote for this quotation.

←   Press 2 times to move directly behind the period in the quotation.

Ctrl F7 , 1   Select the *Create* option on the Footnote menu to create a new footnote. You are placed in a special editing screen for footnotes and endnotes.

TYPE **1984-85 State Big Game Proclamation**

[F7] Exit the editing screen and save the footnote.

```
Permits
        During the 1984 Hunting season the Lone Pine Game

Reserve offered permits for the taking of Deer, Elk,

Antelope, Moose, Buffalo, Rocky Mountain Goat, and

Bighorn Sheep.  The permits were issued by lottery, bid,

and once-in-a-lifetime priorities.  The hunting hours

were continued as per recommendation of the 1983 program

improvement proposal (ANPI-83-LPNP):
                    HUNTING HOURS
        It is unlawful to take big game except
during daylight hours.  Daylight hours are
defined as that period between one-half hour
before official sunrise to one-half hour after
official sunset.1_


B:\REPORT1.LRN                    Doc 1  Pg 3  Ln 29      Pos 37
```

7.5   Split the screen and retrieve

To retrieve a graph from a separate file into the document, it is easiest to split the screen and work with the graph in the lower window.

[Ctrl] [Home] Select the Go To feature.

TYPE **:** (a colon) to move to the colon at the end of the graph statement.

[↓] Move to Line 48 Position 15.

[Ctrl] [F3] , [1] Select the *Window* option on the Screen menu to open a window.

ENTER **6** to split the screen with 6 lines in the upper window.

[Shift] [F3] Switch to the lower window.

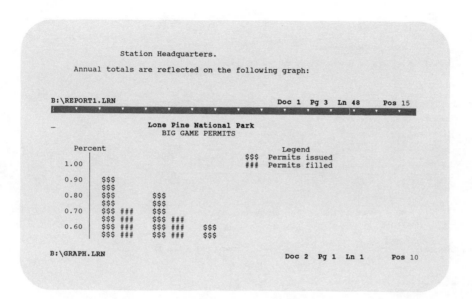

Shift F10　Select the Retrieve feature.

ENTER　**graph.lrn** as the filename for the second document.

Replace

Replace the "$" in the graph with "=".

Alt F2 , N　Select the Replace without confirm feature.

TYPE　**$** for the search string.

F2　Accept the search string. You are asked what should replace the search string.

TYPE　**=** for the replace string.

F2 Start replacing. Every occurrence of "$" is automatically replaced with "=".

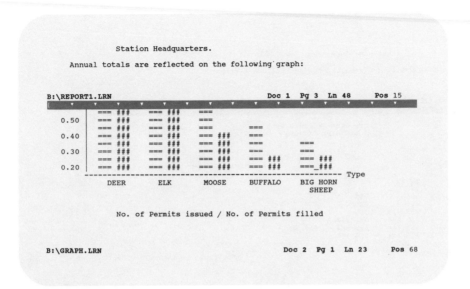

Move the edited graph

Now that you have edited the graph, you are ready to move it into the body of the report.

Home, **Home**, **↑** Move to the top of the graph.

Ctrl **F4**, **3** Select the *Page* option on the Move menu to highlight the graph.

1 Cut the graph from the window.

Shift **F3** Switch to the report in document 1.

Ctrl **F3**, **1** Select the *Window* option on the Screen menu to display the "# Lines in this Window:" message.

ENTER **24** to close the window.

Ctrl **F4** , **5** Select the *Retrieve Text* option on the Move menu to insert the edited graph into the report.

↑ , **Ctrl** **↵** Insert a page break.

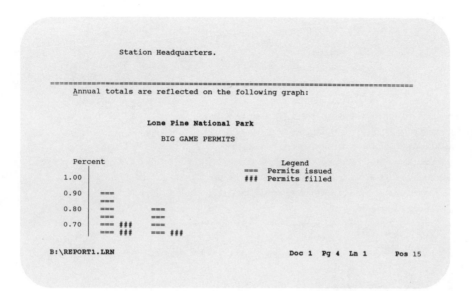

7.8 Restart page numbering

You want page numbering to begin with the body of the report rather than with the title page, so start numbering over on page 3 and place the page numbers in a header.

Ctrl **Home** Select the Go To feature.

ENTER **3** to move to the top of page 3.

Alt **F8** , **2** Select the *New Page Number* option on the Page Format menu to specify a new page number.

ENTER **1** to start the numbering at one.

TYPE **1** for printing Arabic Style numbers.

6 , **1** , **1** Select the *Headers or Footers* option to print a header at the top of every page (beginning on the current page). You are placed in a special editing screen for headers and footers.

Alt **F6** Select the Flush Right feature to place the header at the right margin.

TYPE **Lone Pine Annual Report -**

Space Bar Add a space between the text and the upcoming page number.

Ctrl B	Insert ^B to automatically number pages. ^B is a code that tells WordPerfect to increment the pages in order.
F7 , ↵	Save the header and exit the Page Format menu.

```
                    _              Division I
                              Big Game Reserve


         Permits
                   During the 1984 Hunting season the Lone Pine Game
              Reserve offered permits for the taking of Deer, Elk,
              Antelope, Moose, Buffalo, Rocky Mountain Goat, and
              Bighorn Sheep.  The permits were issued by lottery, bid,
              and once-in-a-lifetime priorities.  The hunting hours
              were continued as per recommendation of the 1983 program
              improvement proposal (ANPI-83-LPNP):
                              HUNTING HOURS

         B:\REPORT1.LRN                        Doc 1  Pg 1  Ln 1      Pos 15
```

7.9   New page number

In numbering the pages of your report, make an allowance for pages to be inserted later. Restart page numbering at 15 on the summary page.

F2	Select the ▶Search feature.
TYPE	**summary** to move to the summary page.
F2	Begin the search. The cursor stops to the right of the first occurrence of "summary."
Home , Home , Home , ←	Move to the left margin before any codes.
Alt F8 , 2	Select the *New Page Number* option on the Page Format menu to specify a new page number.
ENTER	**15** to start the numbering at fifteen.

TYPE **1** for printing Arabic Style numbers.

⏎ Exit the Page Format menu.

```
     Insert Section II  - 3 pages
     Insert Section III - 4 pages
     Insert Section IV - 2 pages
     Insert Program Improvements 1985-86 - 2 pages
========================================================================
Summary
          Because of increased revenues during 1984, the park
     was able to meet most of its outstanding obligations.
     The program improvement proposal for the 1985-86 year
     can, in part, be funded through park revenues.  However,
     the donated funds mentioned in the proposal are needed
     to complete the 1985-86 projects.


     B:\REPORT1.LRN                      Doc 1  Pg 15  Ln 1     Pos 15
```

7.10 | Print and save

Print and save the document, then clear the screen.

Shift F7 , 1 Select the *Full Text* option on the Print menu to print the report.

F7 , Y Begin saving the report.

ENTER **report.2** as the filename.

 Clear the screen.

Text Columns

This lesson guides you through the basic steps of creating the two types of Text Columns. Newspaper-Style Columns are designed for text that is continuous from the bottom of one column to the top of the next (e.g., a newsletter). Parallel Columns are designed to keep items together in columns side-by-side (e.g., inventory item listing).

You may want to turn off Auto-Rewrite while in text columns if the screen rewrites too slowly for you.

In this lesson, you set up both types of columns, then retrieve text into the Newspaper-Style Columns (to save you time), and enter text into Parallel Columns to see the protection feature in action. You also learn how to move through columns and insert additional text.

While working through the lesson, you learn the following facts about WordPerfect's features:

- Text Columns can be Newspaper-Style or Parallel.

- Retrieve can be used in Text Columns.

- Center can be used in Text Columns.

- Go To can be used to move from column to column.

- Parallel Columns are protected from page breaks.

The skills you learn in this lesson can be used to

- Create inventory forms and listings.
- Create scripts and resumes.
- Create a newsletter for your organization.

8.1 Retrieve a document

Retrieve the Campsite Reservation form. This is the document in which you will define columns.

Shift F10 Select the Retrieve feature.

ENTER camps.lrn as the filename.

```
              Lone Pine National Park

                CAMPSITE RESERVATIONS

The Park has four established campgrounds.  Different types of
campsites are available:

     Type A -  Paved/grass with individual water and electric
               hookup
     Type B -  Group of six paved/grass campsites with common
               water/electric hookup
     Type C -  Unpaved with water hookup only
     Type D -  Tent only

The following campgrounds are located on Lone Pine Reservoir and
have access to the boat docks:


The remaining campgrounds are located in the Wilderness Mountain
area and have access to the trail heads:


For reservations contact the appropriate ranger station:


B:\CAMPS.LRN                              Doc 1  Pg 1  Ln 1      Pos 10
```

8.2 Define Newspaper-Style Columns

Before you can retrieve text into a columnar page layout, you must
first set the column definitions.

MOVE To Line 17 Position 10.

↵ Add a blank line.

Alt F7 , 4 Select the *Column Def* option on the Math/Columns menu to begin
defining columns.

Y Select evenly-spaced columns.

ENTER 5 for five spaces between the columns.

↵ Select "1" for Newspaper-Style Columns.

ENTER 2 for two columns.

⏎ Press 4 times to accept the displayed margins for each column and return to the Math/Columns menu.

3 Turn on Newspaper-Style Columns.

```
                    Lone Pine National Park
                    CAMPSITE RESERVATIONS

The Park has four established campgrounds.  Different types of
campsites are available:

        Type A -  Paved/grass with individual water and electric
                  hookup
        Type B -  Group of six paved/grass campsites with common
                  water/electric hookup
        Type C -  Unpaved with water hookup only
        Type D -  Tent only

The following campgrounds are located on Lone Pine Reservoir and
have access to the boat docks:

        _

The remaining campgrounds are located in the Wilderness Mountain
area and have access to the trail heads:


For reservations contact the appropriate ranger station:

B:\CAMPS.LRN                        Col 1  Doc 1  Pg 1  Ln 18    Pos 10
```

8.3   Insert information

Now that you have defined and turned on the columns, you can retrieve information into them.

Shift F6   Turn on centering to center the title for the first column.

TYPE   **Fish Tail Shore** as the title.

⏎ Press 2 times to end centering and return the cursor to the next line, then add a blank line.

Shift F10   Select the Retrieve feature.

ENTER   **fish.lrn** as the filename.

Esc , ↓   Move to the end of the Fish Tail Shore paragraph. The paragraph reformats to fit into the first column.

Ctrl ⏎   Insert a hard page break which moves the cursor to the top of the second column. You can create columns of various lengths by using the Hard Page key.

Shift F6   Turn on centering to center the title for the second column.

TYPE   **White Sands Beach** as the title.

⏎ Press 2 times to end centering and return the cursor to the next line, then add a blank line.

Shift F10 Select the Retrieve feature.

ENTER **sands.lrn** as the filename.

Esc , ↓ Move to the last line of the White Sands Beach paragraph.

Home , → Move to the end of the line.

Alt F7 , 3 Select the *Column On/Off* option on the Math/Columns menu to turn off Newspaper-Style Columns. The cursor returns to the left margin.

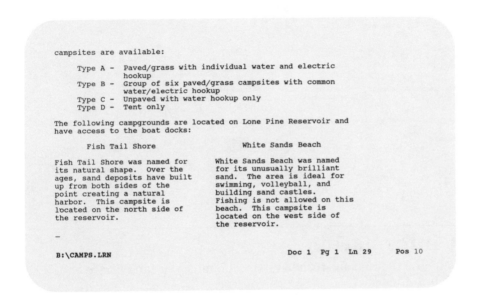

```
campsites are available:

        Type A -  Paved/grass with individual water and electric
                  hookup
        Type B -  Group of six paved/grass campsites with common
                  water/electric hookup
        Type C -  Unpaved with water hookup only
        Type D -  Tent only

The following campgrounds are located on Lone Pine Reservoir and
have access to the boat docks:

        Fish Tail Shore                  White Sands Beach

Fish Tail Shore was named for    White Sands Beach was named
its natural shape.  Over the     for its unusually brilliant
ages, sand deposits have built   sand.  The area is ideal for
up from both sides of the        swimming, volleyball, and
point creating a natural         building sand castles.
harbor.  This campsite is        Fishing is not allowed on this
located on the north side of     beach.  This campsite is
the reservoir.                   located on the west side of
                                 the reservoir.

_

B:\CAMPS.LRN                          Doc 1  Pg 1  Ln 29      Pos 10
```

Now move the cursor to a different place in the document to insert two more pieces of information. This time, insert the information before typing the column titles.

MOVE To Line 32 Position 10.

⏎ Add a blank line.

Alt F7 , 3 Select the *Column On/Off* option from the Math/Columns menu to begin Newspaper-Style Columns. The same column definition as was used in the previous step is used for the following paragraphs.

Shift F10 Select the Retrieve feature.

ENTER **rock.lrn** as the filename.

Esc , 9 , ↓ Move to the end of the Needle Rock paragraph.

Ctrl ⏎ Insert a hard page break which moves the cursor to the top of the second column.

| Shift F10 | Select the Retrieve feature. |

ENTER **silver.lrn** as the filename.

| Esc , 9 , ↓ | Move to the end of the Silver Mine Flats paragraph. |

| Alt F7 , 3 | Select the *Column On/Off* option on the Math/Columns menu to end Newspaper-Style Columns. |

| Esc , 1 , 0 , ↑ | Move the cursor to the top of the first column. Most of the up and down cursor keys move you through the page instead of inside a column. |

| Shift F6 | Turn on centering to center the title for the Needle Rock paragraph. |

TYPE **Needle Rock** as the title.

| ↵ | Press 2 times to end centering and return the cursor to the next line, then add a blank line. |

| ↑ | Press 2 times to move to the title. |

| Ctrl Home , → | Move to the second column. You can use the Go To feature to move from column to column. |

| Shift F6 | Turn on centering to center the title for the Silver Mine Flats paragraph. |

TYPE **Silver Mine Flats** as the title.

| ↵ | Press 2 times to end centering and return the cursor to the next line, then add a blank line. |

```
Fish Tail Shore was named for          White Sands Beach was named
its natural shape.  Over the           for its unusually brilliant
ages, sand deposits have built         sand.  The area is ideal for
up from both sides of the              swimming, volleyball, and
point creating a natural               building sand castles.
harbor.  This campsite is              Fishing is not allowed on this
located on the north side of           beach.  This campsite is
the reservoir.                         located on the west side of
                                       the reservoir.

The remaining campgrounds are located in the Wilderness Mountain
area and have access to the trail heads:

          Needle Rock                         Silver Mine Flats

Needle Rock campground is              Silver Mine Flats campground
surrounded by towering rock            is located at the ghost town
walls.  In the center of the           of Silver Flats City.  It is
campground is a slender rock           the trail head for all the
formation where water has              trails through the wilderness
eroded an eye through the              area.  There are two silver
middle of the rock, giving the         mines that are open daily to
formation the appearance of a          the public.  A back packer's
needle.                                and prospector's dream.

B:\CAMPS.LRN                           Col 2  Doc 1  Pg 1  Ln 35     Pos 45
```

8.4 Define Parallel Columns

Parallel Columns are designed to keep a group of items together in side-by-side columns when working with the Text Columns feature.

Home , Home , ↓ Move to the end of the reservation form.

Alt F7 , 4 Select the *Column Def* option on the Math/Columns menu to define text columns.

N Answer "no" to define your own margins for the text columns.

2 Select "2" for Parallel Columns.

ENTER **3** to specify the number of columns.

ENTER **10**, then **32** for the left and right margins of the first column.

ENTER **35**, then **57** for the left and right margins of the second column.

ENTER **60**, then **82** for the left and right margins of the third column.

3 Begin Parallel Columns.

```
                              the reservoir.

The remaining campgrounds are located in the Wilderness Mountain
area and have access to the trail heads:


        Needle Rock                    Silver Mine Flats

Needle Rock campground is      Silver Mine Flats campground
surrounded by towering rock    is located at the ghost town
walls.  In the center of the   of Silver Flats City.  It is
campground is a slender rock    the trail head for all the
formation where water has      trails through the wilderness
eroded an eye through the      area.  There are two silver
middle of the rock, giving the mines that are open daily to
formation the appearance of a  the public.  A back packer's
needle.                        and prospector's dream.



For reservations contact the appropriate ranger station:

_


B:\CAMPS.LRN                      Col 1  Doc 1  Pg 1  Ln 49     Pos 10
```

8.5 Create the address listing

Now use the Parallel Columns feature to create an address listing for the ranger stations.

TYPE **Ranger Hyrum R. Stone**

Ctrl ↵ Insert a hard page break which moves the cursor to the top of the second column.

TYPE **Reservoir Campgrounds**
Park Headquarters
Lone Pine National Park
Flatwood, Utah 84999

[Ctrl] [↵] Insert a hard page break which moves the cursor to the top of the third column.

TYPE **801 666-5555**

[Ctrl] [↵] Insert a hard page break which moves the cursor back to the first column. Notice that there is no Hard Page code inserted after the third column. This is because WordPerfect automatically ends each group of Parallel Columns with a Column Off code, then turns columns back on.

TYPE **Ranger John Bigney**

[Ctrl] [↵] Insert a hard page break which moves the cursor to the top of the second column.

TYPE **Silver Mine Flats**
Ranger Station
Lone Pine National Park
Flatwood, Utah 84999

Notice that as soon as the page ended, Ranger John Bigney and his address were moved together to the top of page 2. This is because WordPerfect inserts Block Protection codes around each group of columns to keep them protected from a page break.

[Ctrl] [↵] Insert a hard page break which moves the cursor to the top of the third column.

TYPE **801 666-4444**

[Ctrl] [↵] Insert a hard page break which moves the cursor back to the first column.

TYPE **Ranger Jessie Parker**

[Ctrl] [↵] Insert a hard page break which moves the cursor to the top of the second column.

TYPE **Needle Rock**
Ranger Station
Lone Pine National Park
Flatwood, Utah 84999

[Ctrl] [↵] Insert a hard page break which moves the cursor to the top of the third column.

TYPE **801 666-3333**

⊞Ctrl⊞↵ Insert a hard page break which moves the cursor back to the first column. That ends the last group of columns in the listing.

```
formation the appearance of a        the public.  A back packer's
needle.                              and prospector's dream.


For reservations contact the appropriate ranger station:

Ranger Hyrum R. Stone      Reservoir Campgrounds    801 666-5555
                           Park Headquarters
                           Lone Pine National Park
                           Flatwood, Utah 84999

-------------------------------------------------------------------------
Ranger John Bigney         Silver Mine Flats        801 666-4444
                           Ranger Station
                           Lone Pine National Park
                           Flatwood, Utah 84999

Ranger Jessie Parker       Needle Rock              801 666-3333
                           Ranger Station
                           Lone Pine National Park
                           Flatwood, Utah 84999

_

B:\CAMPS.LRN                            Col 1  Doc 1  Pg 2  Ln 11     Pos 10
```

8.6 Margin release

Release the left margin for each of the sentence headings.

MOVE To Page 1 Line 47 Position 10.

⊞Shift⊞ ⊞Tab⊞ Select the ◀Margin Release feature to move the sentence one tab stop to the left of the margin.

MOVE To Line 30 Position 10.

⊞Shift⊞ ⊞Tab⊞ Select the ◀Margin Release feature to move the sentence one tab stop to the left of the margin.

MOVE To Line 15 Position 10.

⊞Shift⊞ ⊞Tab⊞ Select the ◀Margin Release feature to move the sentence one tab stop to the left of the margin.

MOVE To Line 5 Position 10.

Select the ◀Margin Release feature to move the sentence one tab stop to the left of the margin.

```
    The Park has four established campgrounds.  Different types of
        campsites are available:

                Type A -  Paved/grass with individual water and electric
                          hookup
                Type B -  Group of six paved/grass campsites with common
                          water/electric hookup
                Type C -  Unpaved with water hookup only
                Type D -  Tent only

    The following campgrounds are located on Lone Pine Reservoir and
        have access to the boat docks:

                Fish Tail Shore                 White Sands Beach

        Fish Tail Shore was named for    White Sands Beach was named
        its natural shape.  Over the     for its unusually brilliant
        ages, sand deposits have built   sand.  The area is ideal for
        up from both sides of the        swimming, volleyball, and
        point creating a natural         building sand castles.
        harbor.  This campsite is        Fishing is not allowed on this
        located on the north side of     beach.  This campsite is
        the reservoir.                   located on the west side of
                                         the reservoir.

    B:\CAMPS.LRN                              Doc 1  Pg 1  Ln 5     Pos 5
```

8.7   Print and save

Now print and save the reservation form, then clear your screen.

Shift F7 , 1   Select the *Full Text* option on the Print menu to print the reservation form.

F7 , Y   Begin saving the reservation form.

ENTER **camps.1** as the filename.

Clear the screen.

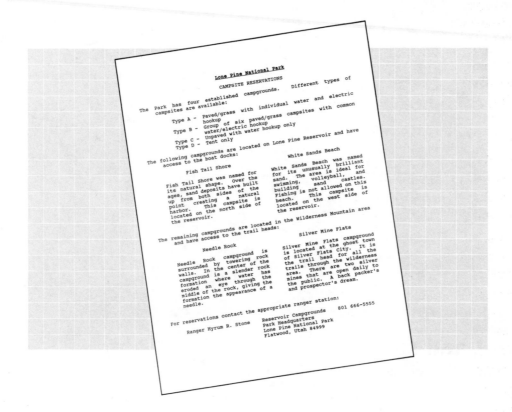

Mail-Merge

Every organization or business frequently sends notices or letters to members, clients, or prospective buyers. The Merge feature in WordPerfect helps you automatically create a *personalized* letter for each person.

In this lesson, you use the Merge feature to create several personalized Letters of Commendation for the Volunteer Fire Department of Flatwood. The secondary file contains all the particular information about each fire fighter. The primary file contains the basic letter. After creating these files, you can start the merge, then sit back as WordPerfect takes over and creates a letter for each fire fighter.

Lessons 30-36 give you more practice with the Merge feature.

While working through the lesson, you learn the following facts about WordPerfect's Merge feature:

• A secondary file contains a record of information about each individual.

• A record is divided into fields by using ^R.

• The primary file contains the form letter itself.

• You can retrieve information into the letter from the secondary file by using ^F.

• The merge creates a letter for each record in the secondary file.

The skills you learn in this lesson about the Merge feature can be used to create

• *Personalized* mass mailings.
• Customer letters.
• Organization notices.
• Contribution solicitations.

9.1 Secondary file

The instructions below help you create a record of information about Alan Wilson that can be stored in a secondary file and used in a merge. The record is divided by ^R's into fields that contain a name, address, etc.

TYPE **Mr. Alan Wilson**

[F9] End the name field with ^R and return the cursor to the next line.

TYPE **Flatwood Market**

[F9] End the business field with ^R and return the cursor to the next line.

TYPE **55 E. Main Street**

⏎ End the first line of the address field with a hard return and return the cursor to the next line. You can have more than one line in a field.

TYPE **Flatwood, Utah 84999**

F9 End the address field with ∧R and return the cursor to the next line.

TYPE **801 666-4545**

F9 End the phone number field with ∧R and return the cursor to the next line.

TYPE **Alan**

F9 End the first name field with ∧R and return the cursor to the next line.

Shift F9 End the record on Alan Wilson with ∧E and return the cursor to the next line.

```
Mr. Alan Wilson^R
Flatwood Market^R
55 E. Main Street
Flatwood, Utah 84999^R
801 666-4545^R
Alan^R
^E
_
```

                                        Doc 1 Pg 1 Ln 8   Pos 10

Now that you understand how to end a field with ∧R and a record with ∧E, type a record for Jeff Richards. Remember to press the Enter key after the street address—not the Merge R key.

TYPE **Mr. Jeff Richards∧R
Flatwood Motors∧R
58090 Bonnie View Court
Flatwood, Utah 84999∧R
801 666-6767∧R
Jeff∧R
∧E**

Notice that Jeff's and Alan's records contain the same number of fields and each field contains the same type of information.

```
Mr. Alan Wilson^R
Flatwood Market^R
55 E. Main Street
Flatwood, Utah 84999^R
801 666-4545^R
Alan^R
^E
Mr. Jeff Richards^R
Flatwood Motors^R
58090 Bonnie View Court
Flatwood, Utah 84999^R
801 666-6767^R
Jeff^R
^E
_
```

Doc 1 Pg 1 Ln 15   Pos 10

You are ready to type the last record in the secondary file.

TYPE **Mr. John Elliot^R**
Wagon Wheel Diner^R
1100 North State Street
Flatwood, Utah 84999^R
^R
John^R
^E

Even though a telephone number is not available for John, ^R still ends the empty field.

```
Mr. Alan Wilson^R
Flatwood Market^R
55 E. Main Street
Flatwood, Utah 84999^R
801 666-4545^R
Alan^R
^E
Mr. Jeff Richards^R
Flatwood Motors^R
58090 Bonnie View Court
Flatwood, Utah 84999^R
801 666-6767^R
Jeff^R
^E
Mr. John Elliot^R
Wagon Wheel Diner^R
1100 North State Street
Flatwood, Utah 84999^R
^R
John^R
^E
_
```

Doc 1   Pg 1   Ln 22   Pos 10

[F7] , [Y]   Begin saving the three records as a secondary file.

ENTER   **address.sf** as the filename.

[↵]   Clear the screen. You have now typed and saved a secondary file.

9.2   Primary file

Once you have created the secondary file, you can retrieve information from specific record fields into a primary file. A primary file can be a form letter like the one you create here.

[Alt] [F9]   Select the Merge Codes feature and a menu appears.

[F] , [1] , [↵]   Insert ^F1^ into the letter. Information from field one (the name field) will be retrieved into the letter.

[↵]   Return the cursor to the next line.

[Alt] [F9]   Select the Merge Codes feature and a menu appears.

[F] , [2] , [↵]   Insert ^F2^ into the letter. Information from field two (the business name field) will be retrieved into the letter.

[↵]   Return the cursor to the next line.

[Alt] [F9]   Select the Merge Codes feature and a menu appears.

⌨ F , ⌨ 3 , ⏎ Insert ^F3^ into the letter. Information from field three (the address field) will be retrieved into the letter.

⏎ Press 2 times to return the cursor to the next line and add a blank line.

Now type the salutation.

TYPE **Dear**

⌨ Space Bar Add a space between "Dear" and the first name.

⌨ Alt ⌨ F9 Select the Merge Codes feature and a menu appears.

⌨ F , ⌨ 5 , ⏎ Insert ^F5^ into the letter. Information from field five (the first name field) will be retrieved into the letter.

TYPE : (a colon).

⏎ Press 2 times to return the cursor to the next line and add a blank line.

```
`F1`
`F2`
`F3`

Dear `F5`:

_


                                          Doc 1  Pg 1  Ln 7     Pos 10
```

Now you can create the body of your letter.

Tab Insert a tab to indent the first line of the paragraph.

TYPE **Thank you,**

Space Bar Insert a space before the first name.

Alt F9 Select the Merge Codes feature and a menu appears.

F , 5 , ⏎ Insert ^F5^ into the letter.

TYPE , (a comma).

Space Bar Insert a space after the comma.

for an outstanding effort in fighting the largest fire in Lone Pine National Park's history. The volunteer fire fighters in your community are an inspiring model for all fire fighters in our state and nation.

With appreciation,

Ranger John T. Smith

```
 ˙F1˙
 ˙F2˙
 ˙F3˙

Dear ˙F5˙:

     Thank you, ˙F5˙, for an outstanding effort in fighting the
largest fire in Lone Pine National Park's history.  The volunteer
fire fighters in your community are an inspiring model for all
fire fighters in our state and nation.

With appreciation,


Ranger John T. Smith_



                                  Doc 1  Pg 1  Ln 16      Pos 30
```

9.3 Begin the merge

After saving the primary file, you are ready to merge the two files.

F7 , Y   Begin saving the letter as a primary file.

ENTER   **letter.pf** as the filename.

↵   Clear the screen.

With the screen clear and both the primary and secondary files on disk, start the merge.

Ctrl F9 , 1   Select the *Merge* option on the Merge/Sort menu.

ENTER   **letter.pf** as the primary file.

ENTER   **address.sf** as the secondary file and the merge begins.

Information from the first record is merged into the letter, then the merge continues on to the second and third records. When the merge is complete, you should have a letter for each record. The letters are separated by Hard Page breaks.

```
Ranger John T. Smith

=================================================================================
Mr. John Elliot
Wagon Wheel Diner
1100 North State Street
Flatwood, Utah 84999

Dear John:

     Thank you, John, for an outstanding effort in fighting the
largest fire in Lone Pine National Park's history.  The volunteer
fire fighters in your community are an inspiring model for all
fire fighters in our state and nation.

With appreciation,


Ranger John T. Smith_




                              Doc 1   Pg 3   Ln 17      Pos 30
```

9.4 Print and save

The three letters you have merged can now be printed and saved in a file of their own.

[Shift] [F7] , [1] Select the *Full Text* option on the Print menu to print the letters.

[F7] , [Y] Begin saving the letters.

ENTER **commend.ltr** as the filename.

⏎ Clear the screen.

Mr. John Elliot
Wagon Wheel Diner
1100 North State Street
Flatwood, Utah 84999

Dear John:

    Thank you, John, for an outstanding effort in fighting the
largest fire in Lone Pine National Park's history. The volunteer
fire fighters in your community are an inspiring model for all
fire fighters in our state and nation.

With appreciation,

Ranger John T. Smith

Lesson 10

 # Memo-Merge

You can *automate* a frequently used form—such as a memo—by using the ^C Merge code and the Merge feature. Each time WordPerfect finds ^C during a merge, the merge pauses to let you enter information from the keyboard.

You can also use the ^O Merge code to display a reminder on your screen of the kind of information you need to enter. All these codes are placed in the primary file. Because the information comes from the keyboard, you do not need a secondary file.

In this lesson, you create and save a primary file that can be used with the Merge feature to quickly produce a memo.

Lessons 30-36 give you more practice with the Merge feature.

While working through the lesson, you learn the following facts about WordPerfect's features:

- The Alignment Character feature lets you change the character for a Tab Align.

- The ^D Merge code inserts the current date during a merge.

- The ^C Merge code lets you delay the merge for information from the keyboard.

- The ^O Merge code lets you display a reminder on the screen.

- You do not need a secondary file if you are merging from the keyboard.

- The Merge R key continues the merge after pausing at ^C.

- The Merge E key can stop a merge which has paused at ^C.

The skills you learn in this lesson can be used to create forms, such as a memo, that can be used in a merge.

10.1 Begin the memo

At the top of the memo, type the title and date.

`Shift` `F6` Turn on centering.

`F6` , `F8` Turn on bolding and underlining.

TYPE **Lone Pine National Park**

`F6` , `F8` Turn off bolding and underlining.

`↵` Press 2 times to turn off centering and return the cursor to the next line, then add a blank line.

Alt F6 Select the Flush Right feature to place the Date entry at the right margin.

TYPE Date:

Space Bar Press 2 times to add space after the Date entry.

Alt F9 , D Select the Merge Codes feature and insert ^D into the memo.

When the merge begins, the current date will be inserted at ^D. The correct date appears only if it was entered when you started your computer.

↵ Press 2 times to add extra blank lines.

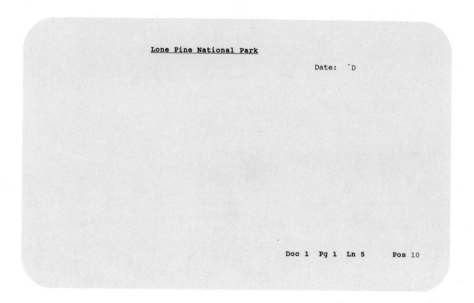

```
                    Lone Pine National Park

                                              Date:  ^D













                                  Doc 1  Pg 1  Ln 5      Pos 10
```

10.2 Alignment character

For memo format, you need to use a colon (:) as the alignment character.

Shift F8 , 6 Select the *Alignment Character* option on the Line Format menu.

TYPE : (a colon).

Alt F3 Display the Reveal Codes screen and notice the [Align Char::] code inserted into the memo.

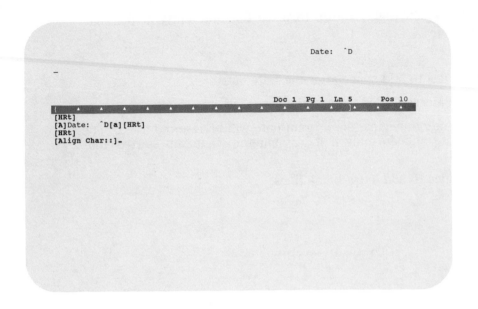

```
                                              Date:  ˆD


      —

                                           Doc 1  Pg 1  Ln 5      Pos 10
{     ▲     ▲     ▲     ▲     ▲     ▲     ▲     ▲     ▲  ]▲     ▲     ▲
[HRt]
[A]Date:   ˆD[a][HRt]
[HRt]
[Align Char::]_
```

⏎   Exit the Reveal Codes screen.

PgUp , PgDn   Scroll through the text to redisplay the memo title on the screen.

10.3   Type the memo headings

Now type the "Reply to," "Subject," and "To" entries in the memo heading.

Tab , Ctrl F6   Insert a Tab, then select the Tab Align feature to begin aligning text at the second tab stop.

TYPE **Reply to:**

When you type the colon, aligning ends and the cursor begins moving to the right again.

Space Bar   Press 2 times to add space after the "Reply to" entry.

Alt F9 , C   Select the Merge Codes feature and insert ^C into the memo.

When the merge begins, WordPerfect stops at ^C to let you enter text from the keyboard.

⏎   Press 2 times to return the cursor to the next line and add a blank line.

Tab , Ctrl F6   Insert a Tab, then select the Tab Align feature to begin aligning text at the second tab stop.

TYPE **Subject:**

Space Bar   Press 2 times to add space after the "Subject" entry.

Alt F9 , C	Select the Merge Codes feature and insert ^C into the memo.
↵	Press 2 times to return the cursor to the next line and add a blank line.
Tab , Ctrl F6	Insert a Tab, then select the Tab Align feature to begin aligning text at the second tab stop.
TYPE	**To:**
Space Bar	Press 2 times to add space after the "To" entry.
Alt F9 , C	Select the Merge Codes feature and insert ^C into the memo.
↵	Press 2 times to return the cursor to the next line and add a blank line.

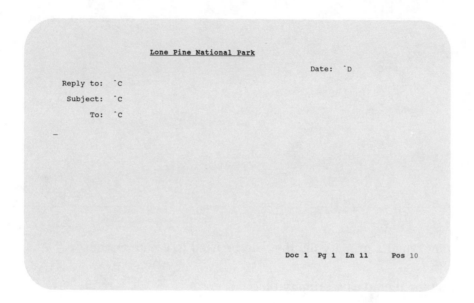

10.4 Complete the memo

Whenever WordPerfect finds ^O during a merge, the text that follows ^O is placed at the bottom of the screen. The text can be a message explaining what needs to be typed when WordPerfect pauses at ^C.

Alt F9 , O	Select the Merge Codes feature and insert ^O into the memo.
TYPE	**Type Memo**
Alt F9 , O	Select the Merge Codes feature and insert ^O into the memo.
Alt F9 , C	Select the Merge Codes feature and insert ^C into the memo.

When WordPerfect finds ^OType Memo^O^C during a merge, the "Type Memo" message will appear at the bottom of the screen and the merge will pause at ^C.

```
                    Lone Pine National Park
                                          Date:  ˆD

        Reply to:  ˆC
         Subject:  ˆC
             To:   ˆC
    ˆOType MemoˆOˆC_




                              Doc 1   Pg 1   Ln 11      Pos 25
```

10.5   Primary file

You have now typed a primary file that can be used to create various memos.

F7 , **Y**   Begin saving the memo as a primary file.

ENTER   **memo** as the filename.

↵   Clear the screen.

10.6   Begin the memo merge

You are now ready to begin the merge. Because the information for the merge comes from the keyboard, you do not need to enter the name of a secondary file.

Ctrl F9 , **1**   Select the *Merge* option on the Merge/Sort menu.

ENTER   **memo** as the primary file.

↵   Begin the merge without a secondary file.

Press the Merge E key at any time to stop the merge and start over. Clear the screen before you start the merge again.

```
                Lone Pine National Park

                                 Date:   August 7, 1984

    Reply to:  _
     Subject:  ^C
          To:  ^C
  ^OType Memo^O^C




  * Merging *                           Doc 1  Pg 1  Ln 5      Pos 23
```

10.7 | Fill in the memo heading

WordPerfect stops at the first ^C.

TYPE **Ranger John T. Smith** for the "Reply to" entry.

F9 Continue the merge.

WordPerfect stops at the second ^C.

TYPE **Fire Restriction** for the "Subject" entry.

F9 Continue the merge.

WordPerfect stops at the third ^C.

TYPE **All Park Entrance Personnel** for the "To" entry.

F9 Continue the merge.

```
              Lone Pine National Park

                            Date:  August, 7, 1984

    Reply to:  Ranger John T. Smith

     Subject:  Fire Restriction

          To:  All Park Entrance Personnel
    _
```

```
Type Memo                        Doc 1  Pg 1  Ln 11    Pos 10
```

10.8 Contents of the memo

WordPerfect displays the "Type Memo" message at the bottom of the screen, then stops at the final $\wedge$C.

TYPE **Effective immediately there will be a fire hazard watch posted for all areas of the park.**

Please warn all visitors that there will be no fires in the park until further notice.

Thank you.

F9 End the merge.

You can use the MEMO primary file as often as you like to create other memos.

```
              Lone Pine National Park

                                 Date:  August 7, 1984

     Reply to:  Ranger John T. Smith

      Subject:  Fire Restriction

           To:  All Park Entrance Personnel

Effective immediately there will be a fire hazard watch posted
for all areas of the park.

Please warn all visitors that there will be no fires in the park
until further notice.

Thank you._




                           Doc 1  Pg 1  Ln 17    Pos 20
```

10.9 Print and save

The memo you have created by merging information from a primary file and the keyboard can now be printed and saved.

Shift F7 , 1 Select the *Full Text* option on the Print menu to print the memo.

F7 , Y Begin saving the memo.

ENTER **memo.1** as the filename.

⏎ Clear the screen.

Lone Pine National Park

Reply to: Ranger John T. Smith   Date: August 7, 1984

Subject: Fire Restriction

To: All Park Entrance Personnel

Effective immediately there will be a fire hazard watch posted for all areas of the park.

Please warn all visitors that there will be no fires in the park until further notice.

Thank you.

Macros

The Macro feature gives you a chance to record a task, then let WordPerfect do the work for you. You can create a macro that sends a document to a particular printer, starts the Speller for you, creates a format, or performs any task that you do frequently.

In this lesson, you use the Macro feature to help you type a closing for a notice from the Lone Pine Ranger Station. Once the closing is inserted, you use another macro to send the notice to the printer.

Lessons 19-22 give you more practice with the Macro feature.

While working through the lesson, you learn the following facts about WordPerfect's Macro feature:

- A macro remembers a series of keystrokes.
- A macro can print a document.
- A macro can close a letter.
- You need to enter the macro name before starting the macro.
- You can use the Alt key to name a macro.

The skills you learn in this lesson can be used to create a macro that will

- Type a letter heading.
- Type a letter closing.
- File and print a document.
- Perform any task that you can do with WordPerfect's features.

11.1   Define a macro

Follow these steps to create a macro that will send one copy of the document on your screen to printer 1.

 Select the Macro Define feature to begin defining the macro. You are asked for the name of the macro you will be defining.

 Use the Alt key to name the macro. The message "Macro Def" begins blinking at the bottom of your screen. From now until you end the macro definition, each key you press will be recorded as part of the macro (even the mistakes!).

 Select the *Full Text* option on the Print menu. These keystrokes to print a document from the screen have now been recorded in the macro.

 Select the Macro Define feature to end defining the macro. The macro is now recorded in a file named ALTP.MAC and the screen is still clear.

Notice that WordPerfect adds a .MAC extension to the filename for you. All macros end with this extension.

11.2 Define a second macro

In this macro, you record a format, text, and some extra spacing.

`Ctrl` `F10` — Select the Macro Define feature to begin defining the macro. You are asked for the name of the macro you will be defining.

ENTER — Your initials (e.g., *JQW*). The "Macro Def" message begins blinking. You are now ready to record the first part of your macro—a tab setting.

`Shift` `F8` , `1` — Select the *Tabs* option on the Line Format menu and the Tab menu appears.

`Ctrl` `End` — Clear all the tab stops (beginning at position 10) from the menu with the Delete EOL feature.

ENTER — **45** for a single left-justified tab at position 45.

`F7` — Exit the Tab menu. The tab setting is recorded and you are ready to begin recording the next part of your macro—the closing.

`Tab` , `Shift` `F6` — Insert a Tab and begin centering around that tab stop.

TYPE — **Sincerely,**

`↵` — Press 4 times to return the cursor to a new line and add blank lines for a signature.

`Tab` , `Shift` `F6` — Insert a Tab and begin centering around that tab stop.

TYPE — **Ranger** and then your own name.

`↵` — Return the cursor to the next line.

`Tab` , `Shift` `F6` — Insert a Tab and begin centering around that tab stop.

TYPE — **Park Director**

Ctrl F10 Select the Macro Define feature to end defining the macro. The macro is recorded in a file that begins with your initials and ends with a .MAC extension.

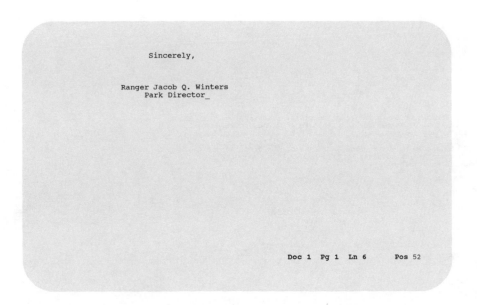

```
                          Sincerely,


                    Ranger Jacob Q. Winters
                         Park Director_
```

                                    Doc 1 Pg 1 Ln 6   Pos 52

F7 , N , ⏎ Clear the screen without saving what's on it, since the information is already recorded in the macro file.

11.3 Use the second macro

Now that both macros are defined, you are ready to use them in a document.

Shift F10 Select the Retrieve feature.

ENTER **notice.lrn** as the filename.

You are going to use the second macro you created to replace the closing on the screen with your own closing to the letter.

MOVE To the "S" in "Sincerely" (Line 20).

Home , Home , Home , ← Move to the beginning of the line before any codes.

Ctrl PgDn , Y Delete text from the cursor position to the end of the page to erase the closing on the screen.

| Alt | F10 | Select the Macro feature and the "Macro:" message appears. |

ENTER   Your initials to start the macro. The new closing appears on the screen.

```
SECOND NOTICE

Joseph R. Hunter
2345 N. Quail Road
Birdseye, Utah 84999

Dear Mr. Hunter,

     This letter is in reference to Citation #89743 issued on 20
October 1984 by Ranger Douglas Lloyd to a Mr. Joseph R. Hunter on
Highway U-83 for possessing more than the legal limit of buffalo.

     According to our records your fine of $5000.00 is past due.
If no response is received by 15 December 1984, you will be
subject to legal action.

                    Sincerely,


                    Ranger Jacob Q. Winters
                        Park Director_



B:\NOTICE.LRN                              Doc 1  Pg 1  Ln 25     Pos 52
```

11.4   Use the first macro

Here you will use the print macro you created to send the letter to the printer before saving it.

| Alt | P | Use the name you assigned to start the macro. The document on the screen is sent to the printer.

Notice that you do not need to use the Macro key to start a macro that is named using the Alt key.

| F7 |, | Y | Begin saving the edited notice.

ENTER **notice.1** as the filename.

⏎ Clear the screen.

Within the letter image:

Lone Pine National Park

SECOND NOTICE

Joseph R. Hunter
2345 N. Quail Road
Birdseye, Utah 84999

Dear Mr. Hunter,

This letter is in reference to **Citation #89743** issued on 20 October 1984 by Ranger Douglas Lloyd to a Mr. Joseph R. Hunter on Highway U-83 for possessing more than the legal limit of buffalo.

According to our records your fine of $5000.00 is past due. If no response is received by 15 December 1984, you will be subject to legal action.

Sincerely,

Ranger Jacob Q. Winters
Park Director

Lesson 12

 File Management

A critical part of word processing is the time you spend taking care of your files. WordPerfect provides you with a List Files feature that displays your files in alphanumeric order. You can then perform a variety of tasks such as retrieving, printing, or copying a file. You can also look into the contents of a file or even search for files that have certain words.

In this lesson, you are given the task of finding a file that has a Tree Harvest Request form and contains Ranger John T. Smith's name. You then change the name to Douglas R. LaRue, copy the file to a formatted diskette, then print the request form from the List Files screen.

You will need an extra, formatted diskette for this lesson.

While working through the lesson, you learn the following facts about WordPerfect's List Files feature:

- List Files lets you create a pattern to display certain files on a diskette or in a directory.

- Word Search helps you find all the files that contain a certain word.

- Look lets you display the contents of a file without retrieving it.

- Retrieve lets you retrieve a file from the List Files screen.

- Copy lets you copy a file to another diskette or directory.

- Rename lets you change the name of a file.

- Print lets you print a file from the List Files screen.

The skills you learn in this lesson can be used to

- Manage the files on a diskette or in a directory.
- Find a file without remembering the filename.
- Make backup copies of files.

12.1 Display a group of files

Before beginning your search for the file with the Tree Harvest Request form, you want to display only those files that might have the form.

F5 Select the List Files feature. The directory displayed should contain your Learning files. If not, type an equal sign (=), then enter the drive or directory before continuing.

ENTER ***.lrn** to display all the files that have a .LRN extension.

The files and information in the List Files illustrations may not exactly match what you see on your screen. However, the keystrokes for each step will still accomplish the outlined task.

```
07/09/86  09:18              Directory B:\*.LRN
Document Size:        0                        Free Disk Space:     77824

. <CURRENT>     <DIR>                    .. <PARENT>      <DIR>
10      .LRN      148   10/25/85 13:33   20      .LRN      154   10/25/85 13:33
30      .LRN      148   10/25/85 13:33   40      .LRN      136   10/25/85 13:33
CAMPS   .LRN      688   10/25/85 13:33   CRAFTS  .LRN      798   10/25/85 13:33
FISH    .LRN      210   10/25/85 13:33   GRAPH   .LRN     1596   10/25/85 13:33
NOTICE  .LRN      584   10/25/85 13:33   PERMITS .LRN     2783   10/25/85 13:33
REPORT  .LRN     3324   10/25/85 13:34   REPORT1 .LRN     3334   10/25/85 13:34
REPORT84.LRN     4865   10/25/85 13:34   ROCK    .LRN      232   10/25/85 13:34
SANDS   .LRN      233   10/25/85 13:34   SILVER  .LRN      256   10/25/85 13:34
TREES   .LRN     1439   10/25/85 13:34




1 Retrieve; 2 Delete; 3 Rename; 4 Print; 5 Text In;
6 Look; 7 Change Directory; 8 Copy; 9 Word Search; 0 Exit: 6
```

12.2 Word Search

You know that the file you are looking for should have Ranger Smith's name and the word "tree" in it. Therefore, do a Word Search for all files with "Smith" and "tree" in them.

9 Select the Word Search feature, and the "Word Pattern:" message appears.

smith;tree to find all the files that have both words. The semicolon serves as an AND operator.

You do not need to type uppercase letters to match a word.

```
07/09/86  09:27              Directory B:\*.LRN
Document Size:        0                         Free Disk Space:    69632

. <CURRENT>    <DIR>                  .. <PARENT>      <DIR>
REPORT1 .LRN    3334  10/25/85 13:34  TREES    .LRN    1439  10/25/85 13:34













1 Retrieve; 2 Delete; 3 Rename; 4 Print; 5 Text In;
6 Look; 7 Change Directory; 8 Copy; 9 Word Search; 0 Exit: 6
```

12.3 Look

You have limited the files to just a few. Now begin using the Look feature to find the file with the request form.

MOVE To the REPORT1.LRN file.

⏎ Select the *Look* option to display the text in the file.

You can use the Page Down key to look through the entire contents of the file. The request form is not in the REPORT1.LRN file.

⏎ Exit the REPORT1.LRN Look screen and return to the List Files screen.

MOVE To the TREES.LRN file.

⏎ Select the *Look* option to display the text in the file.

`PgDn` Move one screen down through the file. The request form is displayed in the TREES.LRN Look screen. You found the correct file!

```
Filename B:\TREES.LRN                                    File Size:    1439
personal or commercial use be able to identify the trees that can
be legally harvested.

     If you are interested in harvesting trees in 1984, fill out
the request form below and send it to:

                    John T. Smith
                    Park Director
                    Lone Pine National Park
                    Fremont, Utah  84666

------------------------------------------------------------------------------

Request for Tree Harvest

Name _____           Date of Harvest _____

Address _____

        _____

Type of tree _____
NOTE: This text is not displayed in WordPerfect format.
Press any key to continue_
```

`↵` Exit the TREES.LRN Look screen and return to the List Files screen.

12.4   Edit the file

You are now ready to substitute Ranger Smith's name with Douglas R. LaRue, then save the new document.

`1` Select the *Retrieve* option.

`Alt` `F2` , `N` Select the Replace without confirm feature.

TYPE **John T. Smith** as the search string to find Ranger Smith's name.

`F2` Accept the search string. You are asked what should replace the search string.

TYPE **Douglas R. LaRue** as the replace string to replace Ranger Smith's name.

F2 Begin replacing. Each occurrence of "John T. Smith" is replaced by "Douglas R. LaRue."

```
        1.   Juniper or Cedar - Needles reduced to little
             green scales on the twigs, cones reduced to
             small bluish berries.

        It is essential that anyone cutting Christmas trees for
   personal or commercial use be able to identify the trees that can
   be legally harvested.

        If you are interested in harvesting trees in 1984, fill out
   the request form below and send it to:

                       Douglas R. LaRue
                       Park Director
                       Lone Pine National Park
                       Fremont, Utah  84666

   ------------------------------------------------------------------

                       Request for Tree Harvest


   Name _____         Date of Harvest

   Address _____

   B:\TREES.LRN                           Doc 1  Pg 1  Ln 28     Pos 31
```

F7 , Y Begin saving the edited document.

ENTER **Larue.bac** as the filename.

↵ Clear the screen.

12.5 Copy to another diskette

Because you want to work with only the LARUE.BAC file, display only that file on the List Files screen.

F5 Select the List Files feature.

ENTER **larue.bac** to display only the LARUE.BAC file.

MOVE To the LARUE.BAC file.

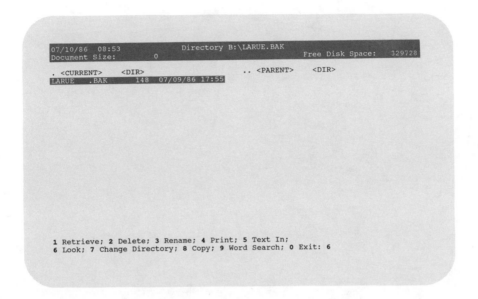

```
07/10/86  08:53             Directory B:\LARUE.BAK
Document Size:        0                      Free Disk Space:    329728

. <CURRENT>   <DIR>                .. <PARENT>    <DIR>
LARUE    .BAK      148  07/09/86 17:55




















1 Retrieve; 2 Delete; 3 Rename; 4 Print; 5 Text In;
6 Look; 7 Change Directory; 8 Copy; 9 Word Search; 0 Exit: 6
```

Since you will be making a backup copy on another diskette, you will need a spare, formatted diskette.

REPLACE Your WordPerfect diskette in drive A with the formatted diskette.

[8] Select the *Copy* option.

If you are running Word-Perfect from a hard disk, place the formatted diskette into drive A.

ENTER **a:** to copy the file where the cursor rests to the formatted diskette in drive A.

REPLACE The formatted diskette with your WordPerfect diskette when copying is complete.

Simply remove the format-ted diskette if you are running WordPerfect from a hard disk.

12.6 Rename and print

Now that you have saved the file on a diskette, you want to rename, then print it.

[3] Select the *Rename* option.

ENTER **larue.trs** as the new filename.

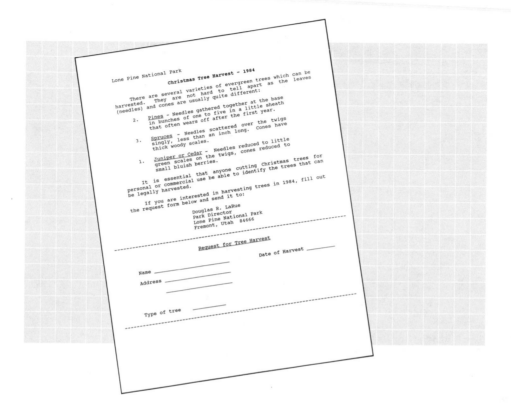

4 Select the *Print* option.

Space Bar Exit the List Files screen.

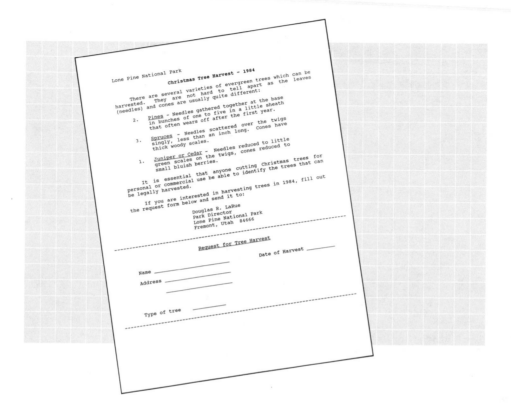

Lone Pine National Park
Christmas Tree Harvest - 1984

There are several varieties of evergreen trees which can be harvested. They are not hard to tell apart as the leaves (needles) and cones are usually quite different:

2. Pines - Needles gathered together at the base in bunches of one to five in a little sheath that often wears off after the first year.

3. Spruces - Needles scattered over the twigs singly, less than an inch long. Cones have thick woody scales.

1. Juniper or Cedar - Needles reduced to little green scales on the twigs, cones reduced to small bluish berries.

It is essential that anyone cutting Christmas trees for personal or commercial use be able to identify the trees that can be legally harvested.

If you are interested in harvesting trees in 1984, fill out the request form below and send it to:

              Douglas R. LaRue
              Park Director
              Lone Pine National Park
              Fremont, Utah 84666

              Request for Tree Harvest

                              Date of Harvest _____

    Name _____
             _____
    Address _____
             _____

    Type of tree _____

Special Features

Thesaurus

The Thesaurus that comes with your WordPerfect package helps you find words with the same meaning as a word in your document. Finding these words can also help you understand the meaning of a word.

In this lesson, you write a sentence that has the right ideas but contains the wrong words. After using the Thesaurus to find synonyms for three of the words, the sentence sounds just as you had hoped.

While working through the lesson, you learn the following facts about WordPerfect's Thesaurus:

• The Thesaurus can look up words already on the screen or words you type in.

• Look Up Word lets you search for synonyms for a word you enter from the keyboard.

• Words being referenced are highlighted in the document. If they are headwords, a list of synonyms appears. If they are not headwords, you are given a chance to enter your own synonym as a headword.

• The Thesaurus looks up synonyms and groups them in grammatical parts of speech.

• Subgroup words labeled with a dot can be referenced as headwords.

• Replace Word replaces the word being referenced with the synonym of your choice.

• You indicate a replacement word by typing the letter (A, B, C,...) associated with it.

• The Moveable menu (A, B, C,...) labels the references under one headword at a time.

• The Right and Left Arrow keys move the Moveable menu from headword to headword.

• Clear Column deletes the references from the column where the Moveable menu stands. The Delete key serves the same function.

The skills you learn in this lesson can be used to find just the right words in any document you create.

13.1 | Start the Thesaurus

Before you can use the Thesaurus, you need to insert the Thesaurus diskette into the proper drive.

If you are running WordPerfect from a hard disk, make sure that TH.WP is in your WordPerfect directory.

REPLACE Your Learning diskette in drive B with the Thesaurus diskette.

TYPE **To blunder is human, to acquit sublime.**

MOVE To the word "blunder," which is the first word you want to replace. The cursor can be anywhere on or just after the word.

To use the Thesaurus to look up a word *not* currently on the screen, start the Thesaurus, type **3**, and enter the word.

If the cursor is not on any word when you start the Thesaurus, you don't need to type a **3**; just enter the word you want to look up.

In this lesson, however, the cursor rests on the word you want to look up, "blunder."

Alt F1 Select the Thesaurus feature to start the Thesaurus.

The menu option numbers at the bottom of the screen and the subgroup numbers in the columns are not related.

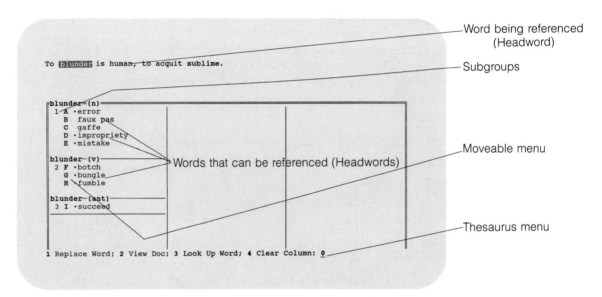

Word being referenced (Headword)

Subgroups

Words that can be referenced (Headwords)

Moveable menu

Thesaurus menu

13.2 Replace "blunder"

The Thesaurus displays synonyms and other words that point to the same idea as the word highlighted on the screen. An acceptable replacement for "blunder" is not on the screen, so move inside this headword to a second level of the Thesaurus list.

TYPE The letter (A, B, C, etc.) next to "mistake" to move to the second level of the Thesaurus list.

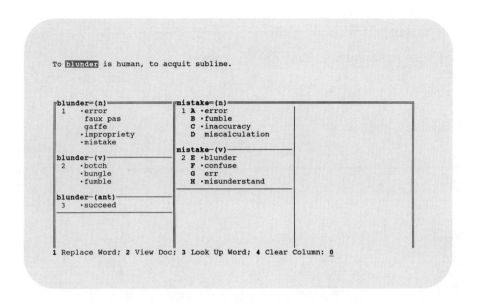

Using "mistake" as a headword, you find the ideal verb to replace "blunder."

1 Select the *Replace Word* option to prepare for the replacement of "blunder" with "err."

TYPE The letter next to "err" and the replacement takes place.

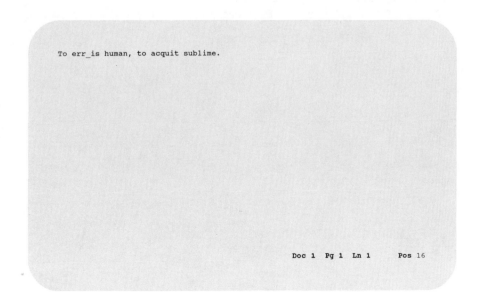

Replace "acquit"

You are now ready to replace "acquit."

MOVE To the word "acquit."

`Alt` `F1` Select the Thesaurus feature to start the Thesaurus.

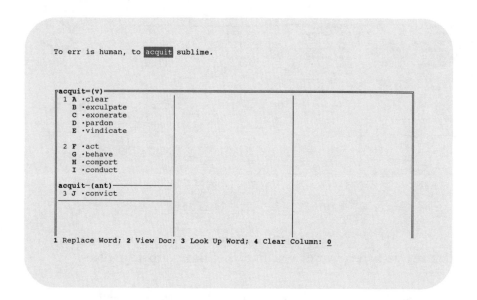

```
To err is human, to acquit sublime.

┌acquit=(v)─────────────────────────────────────────────────────┐
│  1 A •clear                │              │                    │
│    B •exculpate            │              │                    │
│    C •exonerate            │              │                    │
│    D •pardon               │              │                    │
│    E •vindicate            │              │                    │
│                            │              │                    │
│  2 F •act                  │              │                    │
│    G •behave               │              │                    │
│    H •comport              │              │                    │
│    I •conduct              │              │                    │
│acquit-(ant)────────────────┘              │                    │
│  3 J •convict                             │                    │
│                                           │                    │
│                                           │                    │
└───────────────────────────────────────────────────────────────┘
 1 Replace Word; 2 View Doc; 3 Look Up Word; 4 Clear Column: 0
```

TYPE The letter next to "exonerate."

TYPE The letter next to "absolve."

1   Select the *Replace Word* option to prepare for the replacement of "acquit."

TYPE   The letter next to "forgive" and the replacement takes place.

```
To err is human, to forgive_sublime.




                                          Doc 1  Pg 1  Ln 1      Pos 37
```

13.4   Replace "sublime"

The final word you replace is "sublime."

MOVE   To the word "sublime."

Alt F1   Select the Thesaurus feature to start the Thesaurus.

TYPE   The letter next to "divine" to move to the second level of the Thesaurus list.

Del or **4**   Clear the last column (just for fun).

1   Select the *Replace Word* option to prepare for the replacement of "sublime" with "divine."

TYPE The letter next to "divine" and the replacement takes place.

The phrase should now read "To err is human, to forgive divine."

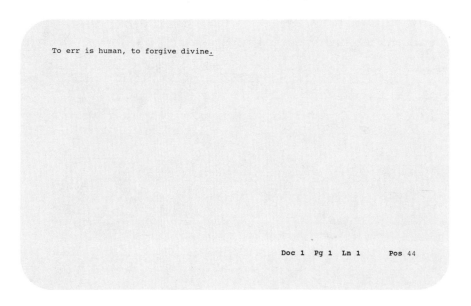

```
To err is human, to forgive divine.

                                        Doc 1  Pg 1  Ln 1      Pos 44
```

If you are using two disk drives, replace the Thesaurus diskette with the Learning diskette before continuing.

Footnotes and Endnotes

Whenever you need to include footnotes or endnotes in any document, from a term paper to a proposal, WordPerfect's Footnote/Endnote feature gives you a quick and easy way to do it.

In this lesson, you create footnotes and endnotes for the Lone Pine Big Game Report, using two different styles.

While working through the lesson, you learn the following facts about WordPerfect's Footnote/Endnote feature:

- Footnotes are numbered and re-numbered automatically.

- WordPerfect adjusts page lengths to accommodate footnotes at the bottom of the page.

- Endnotes are compiled at the end of the document.

- You can quickly change the style of your footnotes/endnotes.

- Footnotes and endnotes can be in the same document.

The skills you learn in this lesson can be used to document your research with footnotes/endnotes.

14.1   Retrieve a document

Retrieve the Lone Pine Big Game report.

   Select the Retrieve feature.

ENTER   **report84.lrn** as the filename.

```
           _                 Lone Pine National Park
                                Big Game Report
                                     1984




                                  Compiled by
                             Ranger John T. Smith
                                Park Director
==============================================================================
                                  PREFACE
                     This report is a summary of the year's activities,
                  as well as goals for the Big Game Reserve of Lone Pine
                  National Park for 1985.



==============================================================================
                                   Permits

B:\REPORT84.LRN                              Doc 1  Pg 1  Ln 1     Pos 10
```

<table>
<tr><td>14.2</td><td>

Create footnotes

</td></tr>
</table>

The exact steps for creating the first footnote are outlined below. Only the document location and text are provided for the second and third footnotes.

MOVE To the end of the first paragraph on page 3.

[Ctrl] [F7] Select the Footnote feature.

```
                                   Permits

          Herd Count

                During the 1984 Hunting season the Lone Pine Game
          Reserve offered permits for the taking of Deer, Elk,
          Antelope, Buffalo, Rocky Mountain Goat, and Bighorn
          Sheep.  A count of all herds as of 31 December 1984
          revealed the current numbers of big game:

                              Big Game Census

                    Antelope. . . . . . . . . . . . .145
                    Big Horn Sheep. . . . . . . . . .250
                    Buffalo. . . . . . . . . . . . . 467
                    Deer. . . . . . . . . . . . . . .1,569
                    Elk. . . . . . . . . . . . . . . 334
                    Rocky Mountain Goat. . . . . . . .98


          Hunting Hours


   1 Create; 2 Edit; 3 New #; 4 Options; 5 Create Endnote; 6 Edit Endnote: 0
```

[1] Select the *Create* option to create a footnote.

[Space Bar] Add a space between the footnote number and the text of the footnote.

TYPE **Ransom A. Grant, "The Uncounted," <u>Rangers in Review</u>, 2 February 1984, pp. 47-49.**

```
        1 Ransom A. Grant, "The Uncounted," Rangers in
Review, 2 February 1984, pp. 47-49._




Press EXIT when done                              Ln 2    Pos 50
```

[F7] Exit the Footnote screen.

MOVE To the end of the second paragraph on page 3.

For the second footnote, follow the basic steps above and type the text below:

TYPE **John L. Winterset, "Program Improvement Report," <u>Government Documents Quarterly</u>, April 1982, pp. 78-92.**

MOVE To the end of the first paragraph on page 5.

For the third footnote, follow the basic steps above and type the text below:

TYPE **Winterset, pp. 78-92.**

14.3 Create endnotes

The exact steps for creating the first endnote are outlined below. Only the document location and text are provided for the second and third endnotes.

MOVE To the end of the last paragraph on page 4.

Ctrl F7 , 5 Select the *Create Endnote* option on the Footnote menu to create an endnote.

F4 Select the ▶Indent feature to indent the endnote text.

TYPE **John R. Last, <u>Tags and Other Wildlife I Have Known</u> (Flatwood: Flatwood Univ. Press, 1984), pp. 23-25.**

F7 Exit the Endnote screen.

MOVE To the end of the first sentence on page 6.

For the second endnote, follow the basic steps above and type the text below:

TYPE **Douglas Lloyd, "The Thrill of It All," <u>Social Hunting Register</u>, 189th ed., (Flatwood: Flatwood Univ. Press, 1982), pp. 33-64.**

MOVE To the end of the paragraph on page 7.

For the third endnote, follow the basic steps above and type the text below:

TYPE **Lloyd, pp. 33-64.**

14.4 Create an endnote page

When endnotes are printed, they appear at the end of the document. Most of the time, you will want them on a separate page, possibly with a title.

Home , Home , ↓ Move to the end of the document.

Ctrl ↵ Insert a Hard Page break to start a new page.

Shift F6 Turn on centering.

F6 , F8 Turn on bolding and underlining.

TYPE **Endnotes** as the title.

F8 , F6 , ↵ Turn off underlining, bolding, and centering.

```
                    receiving the game permit.

           5.    Any violation of the regulation will mean automatic
                 forfeiture of the card (except in "Krivosi
                 Heights").

                 The goals and improvements for the 1985-86 hunts
           are given in detail in the Program Improvements Report.


        ==========================================================================
                                   Summary

                 Because of increased revenues during 1984, due
           largely to Big Game Permits, the park was able to meet
           most of its outstanding obligations.  However, the
           donated funds mentioned in the proposal are needed to
           complete the 1985-86 projects.3


        ==========================================================================
                                   Endnotes


        B:\REPORT84.LRN                      Doc 1  Pg 8  Ln 2      Pos 15
```

14.5 Print

Print the document now to see how the footnotes and endnotes look.

Shift F7 , 1 Select the *Full Text* option on the Print menu to print the Big Game report.

Notice that the footnotes are printed at the bottom of the page, while the endnotes appear on the last page of the document.

Edit a footnote

A date and month need to be changed in the second footnote. By entering the footnote number, WordPerfect finds and displays the footnote you want to edit.

Ctrl F7 , 2   Select the *Edit* option on the Footnote menu to edit a footnote.

ENTER   **2** to edit the second footnote.

MOVE   To the "A" in "April".

Del Press until you delete "April 1982".

TYPE **June 1983**

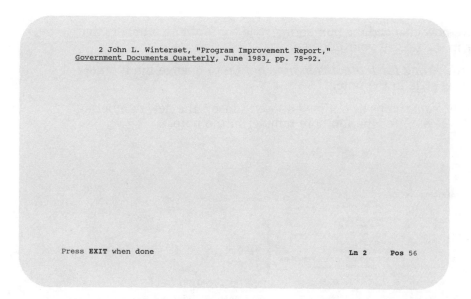

F7 Exit the Footnote screen.

<table>
</table>

14.7   Change numbering styles

A variety of options are available for changing the style of footnote and endnote numbering. For this lesson, change the style for endnotes and footnotes.

Home , **Home** , **↑**   Move to the beginning of the document.

Ctrl **F7** , **4**   Select *Options* from the Footnote menu. The Footnote Options menu appears.

6 , **2**   Select letters for the Endnote numbering mode.

The endnote numbering style has now been changed for endnote numbers in the text of your document.

A   Select the *String for footnotes in text* option to change the footnote numbering style in the text. Now you can customize your own numbering style.

F8   Select the Underline feature to insert an Underline On code [Undrline].

`Ctrl` `F7` , `1` Select the *Footnote/Endnote* option on the Footnote menu to insert a Footnote code in the string.

`F8` Select the Underline feature to insert an Underline Off code [u].

ENTER **/**

You have now changed the numbering style for footnote numbers that appear in the text of your document.

`c` Select the *String for footnotes in note* option to change the footnote numbering style in the note.

Follow the same steps as outlined above to insert the new numbering style (1/, 2/, etc.) for the footnote number in the note.

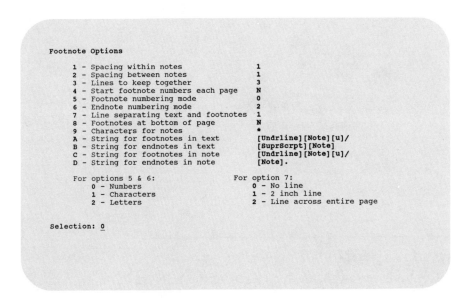

```
Footnote Options

        1 - Spacing within notes              1
        2 - Spacing between notes             1
        3 - Lines to keep together            3
        4 - Start footnote numbers each page  N
        5 - Footnote numbering mode           0
        6 - Endnote numbering mode            2
        7 - Line separating text and footnotes 1
        8 - Footnotes at bottom of page       N
        9 - Characters for notes              *
        A - String for footnotes in text      [Undrline][Note][u]/
        B - String for endnotes in text       [SuprScrpt][Note]
        C - String for footnotes in note      [Undrline][Note][u]/
        D - String for endnotes in note       [Note].

        For options 5 & 6:          For option 7:
            0 - Numbers                 0 - No line
            1 - Characters              1 - 2 inch line
            2 - Letters                 2 - Line across entire page


    Selection: 0
```

`↵` Exit the Footnote Options menu.

14.8 Print

Print the report again and notice the changes in numbering style for the footnotes and endnotes in the text and in the notes.

Shift F7 , 1 Select the *Full Text* option on the Print menu to print the edited Big
Game report.

Redline and Strikeout

When editing a document, you may want to mark the text you want added and/or the text you want deleted. You can use the Redline feature to mark text to be added, and the Strikeout feature to mark text to be deleted.

In this lesson, you take a paragraph of the Lone Pine Big Game report and mark text for Redline and Strikeout, then use the Remove feature to delete the strikeout text and remove the redline markings.

While working through the lesson, you learn the following facts about WordPerfect's Redline/Strikeout feature:

• Redline puts a vertical bar in the margin to note where text has been added.

• Strikeout puts dashes through the letters of the words you want removed from the text.

• Remove takes out the vertical bars and deletes the strikeout text when you get ready to print a final copy.

• Redlined text remains in the document after you use the Remove feature; only the codes and the strikeout text are deleted.

The skills you learn in this lesson can be used to

• Highlight new text for editing approval.
• Highlight text you may want deleted from the final copy.
• Remove the text you don't want.

15.1 Retrieve a document

Retrieve the Lone Pine Big Game report for editing.

Select the Retrieve feature.

ENTER **report84.lrn** as the filename.

```
                    Lone Pine National Park
                       Big Game Report
                           1984




                         Compiled by
                     Ranger John T. Smith
                       Park Director
==============================================================================
                           PREFACE

            This report is a summary of the year's activities,
        as well as goals for the Big Game Reserve of Lone Pine
        National Park for 1985.



==============================================================================
                           Permits

B:\REPORT84.LRN                        Doc 1  Pg 1  Ln 1      Pos 10
```

15.2 Insert a sentence

You want to insert an additional sentence into a paragraph, and mark it for editing approval.

MOVE To the beginning of the second sentence in the paragraph on page 7.

Alt F5 , 3 Select the *Redline* option on the Mark Text menu to begin redlining. A plus sign (+) appears in the status line, next to the position (Pos) number, as a reminder that you are redlining now.

TYPE **The program improvement proposal for the 1985-86 year can be funded in part through park revenues.**

Space Bar Press 2 times to add space between the sentences.

⌨ Alt F5 , 3 Select the *Redline* option on the Mark Text menu to end redlining.

⌨ Ctrl F3 Press 2 times to reformat the screen.

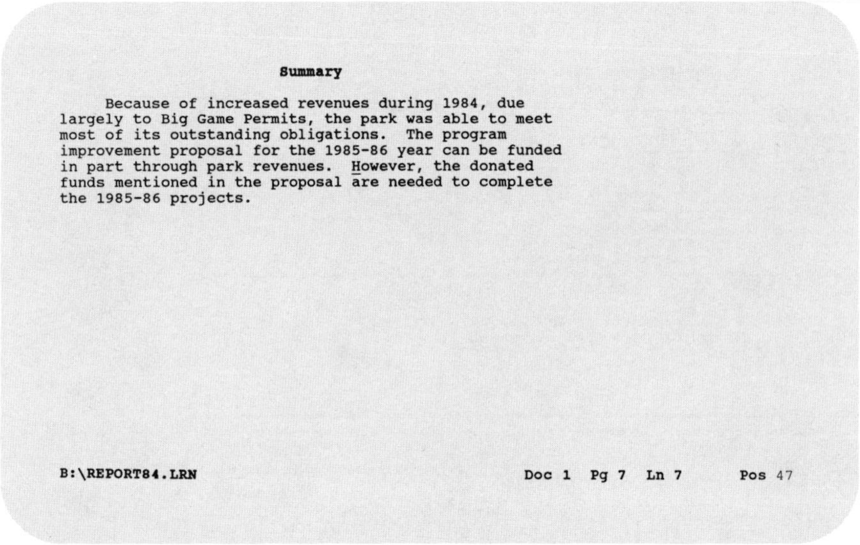

Summary

Because of increased revenues during 1984, due largely to Big Game Permits, the park was able to meet most of its outstanding obligations. The program improvement proposal for the 1985-86 year can be funded in part through park revenues. However, the donated funds mentioned in the proposal are needed to complete the 1985-86 projects.

B:\REPORT84.LRN   Doc 1 Pg 7 Ln 7   Pos 47

15.3 Strikeout a phrase

You want to strikeout a phrase in the report for deletion in the final document.

MOVE To the beginning of the phrase "due largely to..." in the first sentence of the paragraph.

Alt F4 Turn on Block.

TYPE A comma (,) then a space to highlight the phrase.

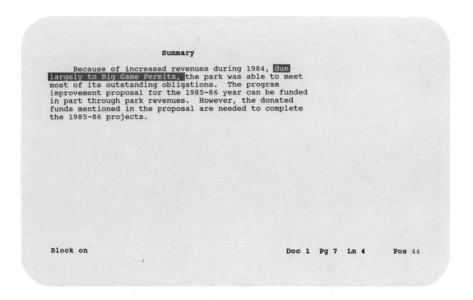

Summary

Because of increased revenues during 1984, due largely to Big Game Permits, the park was able to meet most of its outstanding obligations. The program improvement proposal for the 1985-86 year can be funded in part through park revenues. However, the donated funds mentioned in the proposal are needed to complete the 1985-86 projects.

Block on   Doc 1   Pg 7   Ln 4   Pos 44

Alt F5 , 4 Select the *Strikeout* option on the Block Mark Text menu to strikeout the highlighted phrase.

15.4 Print

You now want to print the paragraph and send it through for approval before printing the final document.

BLOCK The edited paragraph.

Shift F7 , Y Answer "yes" to print the highlighted text. Notice the vertical dash marks in the left margin for the redlined sentence, and the dashes in the strikeout phrase.

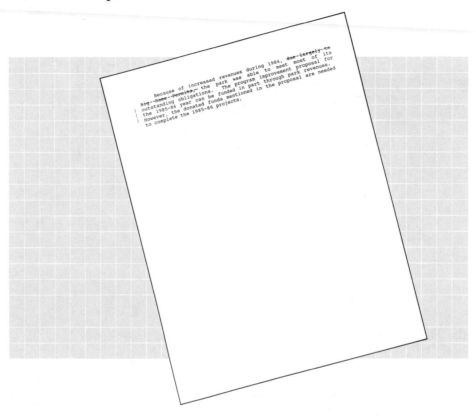

F1 Turn off Block

15.5 Remove

The changes have been approved; you are ready to remove the redline markings and delete the strikeout phrase.

[Alt] [F5] , [6] Select *Other Options* from the Mark Text menu.

[6] Select the Remove feature.

```
                    Summary

     Because of increased revenues during 1984, due
largely to Big Game Permits, the park was able to meet
most of its outstanding obligations.  The program
improvement proposal for the 1985-86 year can be funded
in part through park revenues.  However, the donated
funds mentioned in the proposal are needed to complete
the 1985-86 projects.




Delete Redline markings and Strikeout text? (Y/N) N
```

[Y] Answer "yes" to begin removing the marks and text. Redlined text remains—only the codes are removed. However, both strikeout codes and text are deleted.

15.6 Print

Print the edited page and notice that the redline marks and the strikeout text are gone.

Shift F7 , 2 Select the *Page* option on the Print menu to print the edited page.

Summary

Because of increased revenues during 1984, the park was able to meet most of its outstanding obligations. The program improvement proposal for the 1985-86 year can be funded in part through park revenues. However, the donated funds mentioned in the proposal are needed to complete the 1985-86 projects.

Outline and Paragraph Numbering

The Outline feature in WordPerfect lets you create an outline which is automatically numbered for you.

In this lesson, you create and edit an outline for the Lone Pine Big Game report.

While working through the lesson, you learn the following facts about WordPerfect's Outline feature:

- Outline automatically numbers entries.

- You can have up to seven levels of numbering in your outline.

- When you edit an outline, WordPerfect automatically changes the numbering for you.

The skills you learn in this lesson can be used to quickly create flexible outlines for various purposes.

 16.1 ## Begin the outline

The Outline feature will automatically insert paragraph numbers for you.

[Alt] [F5] , [1] Select the *Outline* option on the Mark Text menu to begin outlining. Notice the "Outline" message on the status line.

```
Outline                          Doc 1  Pg 1  Ln 1      Pos 10
```

Outline

The keystrokes below guide you through creating the first part of the outline.

⏎ Insert the first paragraph number in the first outlining level.

F4 Select the ▶Indent feature to indent the line.

TYPE **Permits** as the first item in the outline.

⏎ Press 2 times to end the indent and return the cursor to the next line, then add a blank line and insert the next paragraph number.

Tab , F4 Insert a Tab to move the paragraph number to the second outlining level, then select the ▶Indent feature to indent the line.

TYPE **Hunting Hours** as the second item in the outline.

⏎ , Tab , F4 Insert a paragraph number, move it to the second outlining level and indent the line.

TYPE **Tags** as the third item in the outline.

⏎ Insert a paragraph number.

Tab Press 2 times to move the paragraph number to the third outlining level.

F4 Select the ▶Indent feature to indent the line.

TYPE **Checking Stations** as the fourth item in the outline.

⏎ Insert a paragraph number.

Tab Press 2 times to move the paragraph number to the third outlining level.

F4 Select the ▶Indent feature to indent the line.

TYPE **Permits and Tags** as the fifth item in the outline.

⏎ Press 2 times to insert a paragraph number and add a blank line.

If you make a mistake, use the Backspace key to delete the text and Paragraph Number code (if necessary). Press the Enter key, or select the Para # option on the Mark Text menu to insert a new code.

```
    I.   Permits

         A.   Hunting Hours
         B.   Tags
              1.   Checking Stations
              2.   Permits and Tags

    II._




    Outline                              Doc 1  Pg 1  Ln 9      Pos 13
```

16.3 Complete the outline

Now that you have learned the basic steps of creating an outline, continue using the Tab, ▶Indent, and Enter keys to create the rest of the outline as shown below:

II.   Big Game Hunts

    A. Conservation Measures
        1. Age Limit
        2. Deer and Elk
    B. Number Taken

III. Hunter Education

IV.   Summary

When you finish creating the outline,

`Alt` `F5` , `1` Select the *Outline* option on the Mark Text menu to end outlining.

```
I.   Permits

     A.   Hunting Hours
     B.   Tags
          1.   Checking Stations
          2.   Permits and Tags

II.  Big Game Hunts

     A.   Conservation Measures
          1.   Age Limit
          2.   Deer and Elk
     B.   Number Taken

III. Hunter Education

IV.  Summary_




                              Doc 1  Pg 1  Ln 18      Pos 22
```

16.4 Print the outline

Now that the outline is complete, send it to the printer.

⌗Shift⌗ ⌗F7⌗ , ⌗1⌗ Select the *Full Text* option on the Print menu to send the outline to the printer.

16.5   Add an entry

Once an outline is created, you might need to edit the text or add new entries. In this step, add a "Herd Count" entry to the outline.

MOVE To the left margin of Line 4.

⌗←⌗ , ⌗↑⌗ Add a blank line and move the cursor to that line.

⌗Tab⌗ Insert a Tab to move to the next tab stop, in line with the second outlining level.

⌗Alt⌗ ⌗F5⌗ , ⌗2⌗ Select the *Para #* option on the Mark Text menu to insert a paragraph number.

⌗←⌗ Insert an automatic paragraph number. This is the same type of paragraph number that the Outline feature inserted for you automatically.

⌗F4⌗ Select the ◗Indent feature to indent the line.

TYPE **Herd Count** as the additional item in the outline.

`Ctrl` `F3` Press 2 times to rewrite the screen and update the paragraph numbers.

```
        I.    Permits

              A.    Herd Count_
              B.    Hunting Hours
              C.    Tags
                    1.    Checking Stations
                    2.    Permits and Tags

        II.   Big Game Hunts

              A.    Conservation Measures
                    1.    Age Limit
                    2.    Deer and Elk
              B.    Number Taken

        III.  Hunter Education

        IV.   Summary




                                   Doc 1  Pg 1  Ln 4      Pos 30
```

16.6 Select the Legal style

Once an outline is created, you can quickly change the style of numbering for the whole outline by inserting a new definition.

`PgUp` Move to the top of the page.

`Alt` `F5` , `6` Select *Other Options* from the Mark Text menu.

`1` Display the Paragraph Numbering Definition menu.

A large menu is displayed on the screen. At the top of the menu is a list of all the preset styles. At the bottom of the menu is a list of options available for creating your own style.

[3] Select the Legal Numbering style.

[↵] Start paragraph numbering at level 1.

[Ctrl] [F3] Press 2 times to rewrite the screen and display the new style in the outline.

```
I.    Permits

      1.1. Herd Count
      1.2. Hunting Hours
      1.3. Tags
            1.3.1.    Checking Stations
            1.3.2.    Permits and Tags

2.    Big Game Hunts

      2.1. Conservation Measures
            2.1.1.    Age Limit
            2.1.2.    Deer and Elk
      2.2. Number Taken

3.    Hunter Education

4.    Summary




                                    Doc 1  Pg 1  Ln 1      Pos 10
```

16.7 Create a new style

Besides selecting from the available styles, you can select from several options to create your own numbering style.

[Back-space] , [Y] Delete the [Par#Def] code for the Legal style.

[Alt] [F5] , [6] Select *Other Options* from the Mark Text menu.

[1] Display the Paragraph Numbering Definition Menu.

[4] Create your own style.

[↵] Press 3 times to accept the current number and punctuation style for level 1, and the number style for level 2.

[2] Select a parenthesis for the level 2 punctuation style.

[1] Select Lower Case Roman for the level 3 number style.

[3] Select parentheses for the level 3 punctuation style.

⮐ Press until you exit the Paragraph Numbering Definition menu.

Ctrl F3 Press 2 times to rewrite the screen and display the new style in the outline.

```
I.   Permits

     A)   Herd Count
     B)   Hunting Hours
     C)   Tags
          (i)   Checking Stations
          (ii) Permits and Tags

II.  Big Game Hunts

     A)   Conservation Measures
          (i)   Age Limit
          (ii) Deer and Elk
     B)   Number Taken

III. Hunter Education

IV.  Summary




                                        Doc 1  Pg 1  Ln 1        Pos 10
```

Table of Contents, Lists, and Index

When writing a report, you will often have need of a table of contents, lists of graphs, illustrations, etc., and/or an index. WordPerfect provides a feature that automatically generates these after you mark which text you want included. All of these features are on the Mark Text menu.

This lesson takes you through the complete process of creating a table of contents, two lists, and an index. You also change the numbering style and generate these tables again.

While working through this lesson, you learn the following facts about WordPerfect's features:

- The Block key highlights text for a table of contents and lists.

- The table of contents can have up to five levels.

- [Mark] and [EndMark] codes are placed before and after the text marked for a table of contents and lists.

- You can mark the text for the index with or without the Block key.

- You can choose from five numbering styles for the table of contents, lists, and index.

- In the table of contents, you can select a different numbering style for each of the five levels.

- Once you mark the text and choose the numbering style, WordPerfect automatically generates a table, list, and index.

The skills you learn in this lesson can be used to

- Create a table of contents for your report.
- Create lists of graphs, maps, illustrations, etc.
- Create an index for your report.

17.1 Retrieve a document

Retrieve the Big Game report for editing.

Select the Retrieve feature.

ENTER **report84.lrn** as the filename.

```
                    Lone Pine National Park
                      Big Game Report
                           1984




                          Compiled by
                      Ranger John T. Smith
                        Park Director
=================================================================
                           PREFACE
         This report is a summary of the year's activities,
       as well as goals for the Big Game Reserve of Lone Pine
       National Park for 1985.



=================================================================
                           Permits

B:\REPORT84.LRN                        Doc 1  Pg 1  Ln 1      Pos 10
```

17.2 Mark text for the table of contents

You are ready to mark text for a two-level table of contents. For the first level,

MOVE To the "Permits" heading at the top of page 3.

BLOCK The heading.

 Select the *ToC* option on the Mark Text menu.

TYPE **1** to mark the heading for level 1 in the table.

Repeat these steps for:

"Big Game Hunts" at the top of Page 5
"Hunter Education Program" at the top of Page 6
"Summary" at the top of Page 7

Once you complete marking the text for the first level of the table, you are ready to mark text for the second level. Move your cursor to the text in the following list and repeat the above steps. This time type **2** for the level number.

"Herd Count" on Page 3 Line 4
"Hunting Hours" on Page 3 Line 23
"Tags" on Page 4 Line 1
"Conservation Measures" on Page 5 Line 4
"Number Taken" on Page 5 Line 16

17.3 Mark text for two lists

You are now ready to mark text for two lists—Tables (list 1) and Graphs (list 2). For the first list,

MOVE To the "Big Game Census" title on Page 3 Line 13.

BLOCK The title.

Alt F5 , 2 Select the *List* option on the Mark Text menu.

TYPE **1** to mark the title for list 1.

Repeat these steps for:

"Hunting Hours" on Page 3 Line 29
"Big Game Tags" on Page 4 Line 19

You are ready to mark an entry for the second list.

MOVE To the "Big Game Hunt" title on Page 5 Line 22.

BLOCK The title.

Alt F5 , 2 Select the *List* option on the Mark Text menu.

```
                    Big Game Hunts


     Conservation Measures

          According the 1983 proposal the Game Reserve would
     conserve the Big Game resources by reducing the number
     of permits available in 1984.  The permits were cut by
     20% for the 1984 hunting season by raising the legal age
     for hunters of big game.  No hunting license (except for
     Rocky Mountain Goat) was issued to any resident under
     the age of twenty-one (21) according to the State Big
     Game Proclamation.


     Number Taken

          The following is a graph of the numbers of big game
     legally taken during the 1983 and 1984 seasons:


                    Big Game Hunt



     List #: _
```

TYPE **2** to mark the title for list 2.

17.4 Mark text for the index

The first task in marking text for the index is to create an "Animals" heading and use each animal name as a subheading.

MOVE To the word "Antelope" in the "Hunting Hours" table at the bottom of page 3.

Alt F5 , 5 Select the *Index* option on the Mark Text menu.

ENTER **Animals** for the heading.

↵ Use the animal name for the subheading.

Follow the above steps for each animal in the list. For multiple-word headings, like Big Horn Sheep and Rocky Mountain Goat, use the Block key to mark the text. When you are finished,

MOVE To "Deer" at the bottom of the graph on Page 5 (Line 45).

Alt F5 , 5 Select the *Index* option on the Mark Text menu.

ENTER **Animals** for the heading.

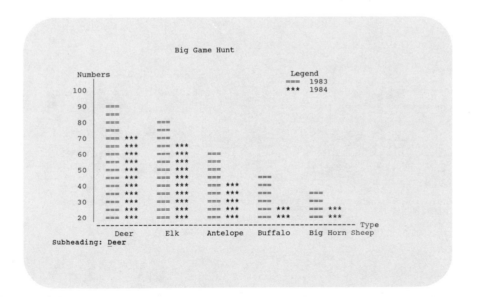

```
                              Big Game Hunt


              Numbers                              Legend
                                                   ===   1983
         100  |                                    ***   1984

          90  | ===
              | ===
          80  | ===      ===
              | ===      ===
          70  | === ***  ===
              | === ***  === ***
          60  | === ***  === ***  ===
              | === ***  === ***  ===
          50  | === ***  === ***  ===
              | === ***  === ***  ===      ===
          40  | === ***  === ***  === ***  ===
              | === ***  === ***  === ***  ===      ===
          30  | === ***  === ***  === ***  ===      ===
              | === ***  === ***  === ***  === ***  === ***
          20  | === ***  === ***  === ***  === ***  === ***
              ----------------------------------------------------- Type
                   Deer      Elk    Antelope  Buffalo  Big Horn Sheep
        Subheading: Deer
```

↵ Use the animal name for the subheading.

Follow the above steps to mark each animal at the bottom of the graph. For Big Horn Sheep, use the Block key to mark the text.

After marking the animal names for indexing, you are ready to mark the text for the "Documents, Government" heading.

To the "ANPI-83-LPNP" reference on Page 3 Line 26.

BLOCK	ANPI-83-LPNP.
Alt F5 , 5	Select the *Index* option on the Mark Text menu.
ENTER	**Documents, Government** for the heading.
↵	Use the displayed text for the subheading.
MOVE	To the end of the first paragraph on page 5.
Alt F5 , 5	Select the *Index* option on the Mark Text menu.
ENTER	**Documents, Government** for the heading.
ENTER	**State Big Game Proclamation** for the subheading.

Now that you are familiar with marking text for an index, move to the beginning of the report and mark each occurrence of "herds" and "Big Game Permits" (you will need to use the Block key for "Big Game Permits"). Press the Enter key for each heading to use the displayed text. There are no subheadings, so press the Enter key again when you see the "Subheading:" message.

Now that you have marked the text you want in each table, list, and index, you are ready to define the numbering style for the table of contents, lists, and index entries in the Lone Pine Big Game report.

17.5 Define the table style

You want to create a title for the table of contents, then define the numbering style.

MOVE	To the end of page 1.
Ctrl ↵	Insert a Hard Page break.
Shift F6 , F6	Turn on centering and bolding.
TYPE	**Table of Contents**
F6	Turn off bolding.
↵	Press 2 times to end centering and return the cursor to the next line, then add a blank line.
Alt F5 , 6	Select *Other Options* from the Mark Text menu.
2	Display the Table of Contents Definition menu.

TYPE **2** for the number of levels in the table.

TYPE **n** to indicate no wrapping for the second level.

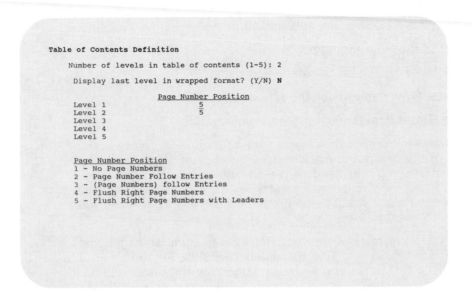

↵ Press 2 times to accept the displayed styles for both levels and exit the menu.

17.6 Define the lists style

There are two lists to define—one for the tables in the report and one for the graphs.

Ctrl ↵ Insert a Hard Page break after the table of contents definition.

Shift F6 , F6 Turn on centering and bolding.

TYPE **Tables** for the first list.

F6 Turn off bolding.

↵ Press 2 times to end centering and return the cursor to the next line, then add a blank line.

Alt F5 , 6 Select *Other Options* from the Mark Text menu.

3 Select the *Define List* option from the menu.

1 , 3 Define the first list for page numbers to follow each entry in parentheses.

You are now ready to define the second list for any graphs in the report.

↵ Press 2 times to add blank lines between the Table and Graph lists.

`Shift` `F6` , `F6` Turn on centering and bolding.

TYPE **Graphs** for the second list.

`F6` Turn off bolding.

`↵` Press 2 times to end centering and return the cursor to the next line, then add a blank line.

`Alt` `F5` , `6` Select *Other Options* from the Mark Text menu.

```
Other Mark Text Options
    1 - Define Paragraph/Outline Numbering
    2 - Define Table of Contents
    3 - Define List
    4 - Define Table of Authorities
    5 - Define Index
    6 - Remove all Redline Markings and all Strikeout text from document
    7 - Edit Table of Authorities Full Form
    8 - Generate Tables and Index




Selection: 0
```

`3` Select the *Define List* option from the menu.

`2` , `5` Define the second list for page numbers flush right with a dot leader.

17.7 Define the index style

The final step before generating the documents is to define the index for the report.

`Home` , `Home` , `↓` Move to the end of the report.

`Ctrl` `↵` Insert a Hard Page break.

`Shift` `F6` , `F6` Turn on centering and bolding.

TYPE **Index** for the index heading.

`F6` Turn off bolding.

`↵` Press 2 times to end centering and return the cursor to the next line, then add a blank line.

`Alt` `F5` , `6` Select *Other Options* from the Mark Text menu.

`5` Select the *Define Index* option from the menu.

`↵` Choose not to use a concordance file.

```
Index Definition

1 - No Page Numbers
2 - Page Numbers Follow Entries
3 - (Page Numbers) Follow Entries
4 - Flush Right Page Numbers
5 - Flush Right Page Numbers with Leaders













Selection: 0
```

`2` Define the index for page numbers to follow each entry.

17.8 Generate the table, lists, and index

With the text marked and the definitions created, you are ready to let
WordPerfect take over and automatically create a table, two lists, and
an index.

`Alt` `F5` , `6` Select *Other Options* from the Mark Text menu.

`8` Begin generating.

`Y` Answer "yes" to indicate that any previously generated documents can
be replaced.

*If your computer does not
have enough memory
available, WordPerfect may
ask you to clear the
Document 2 screen before
generating the tables. Clear
the second screen and start
again.*

A counter keeps you posted on the progress. When WordPerfect is finished, scroll through the report to see the generated text, then print the report.

Shift F7 , 1 Select the *Full Text* option on the Print menu to print the report.

17.9 Change numbering styles

Before printing the final report, try changing the numbering styles for the table of contents and index.

MOVE To the top of page 2.

Alt F3 Display the Reveal Codes screen.

MOVE To the right of the [DefMark:ToC,2] code.

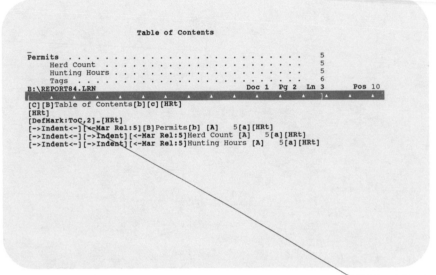

```
                      Table of Contents

Permits . . . . . . . . . . . . . . . . . . . . . . . . . .    5
     Herd Count . . . . . . . . . . . . . . . . . . . . . .    5
     Hunting Hours . . . . . . . . . . . . . . . . . . . . .   5
     Tags . . . . . . . . . . . . . . . . . . . . . . . . .    6
B:\REPORT84.LRN                           Doc 1  Pg 2  Ln 3        Pos 10
                                                                              
[C][B]Table of Contents[b][c][HRt]
[HRt]
[DefMark:ToC,2]-[HRt]
[->Indent<-][<-Mar Rel:5][B]Permits[b] [A]     5[a][HRt]
[->Indent<-][->Indent][<-Mar Rel:5]Herd Count [A]     5[a][HRt]
[->Indent<-][->Indent][<-Mar Rel:5]Hunting Hours [A]     5[a][HRt]
```

Table of Contents Definition code

Back-space Delete the [DefMark:ToC,2] code and the table of contents definition you selected is gone.

Space Bar Exit the Reveal Codes screen.

Alt F5 , 6 Select *Other Options* on the Mark Text menu.

2 Select the *Define Table of Contents* option from the menu.

2 , Y Define two levels for the table of contents, with the second level in a wrapped format.

↵ Press 2 times to accept the displayed numbering styles and exit the menu.

You also want to change the index numbering style to print the page numbers flush to the right margin.

MOVE To the last page.

[Alt] [F3] Display the Reveal Codes screen.

MOVE To the right of the [DefMark:Index,2] code.

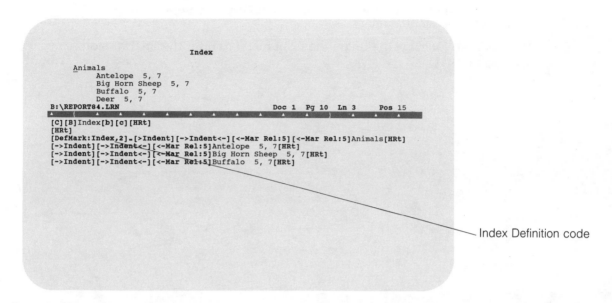

Index Definition code

[Back-space] Delete the [DefMark:Index,2] code and the index definition you selected is gone.

[Space Bar] Exit the Reveal Codes screen.

[Alt] [F5], [6] Select *Other Options* from the Mark Text menu.

[5] Select the *Define Index* option from the menu.

[↵] Choose not to use a concordance file.

[4] Define flush right page numbers for the index.

17.10 | Generate

You are now ready to generate the final table of contents, lists, and index for the report.

[Alt] [F5], [6] Select *Other Options* from the Mark Text menu.

[8] Begin generating.

[Y] Replace the old table of contents, lists, and index.

Follow the progress of generating by watching the counter at the bottom of the screen.

Print the document

After WordPerfect finishes generating the table of contents, lists, and index, print the document.

Shift F7 , 1 Select the *Full Text* option on the Print menu to print the final version of the report.

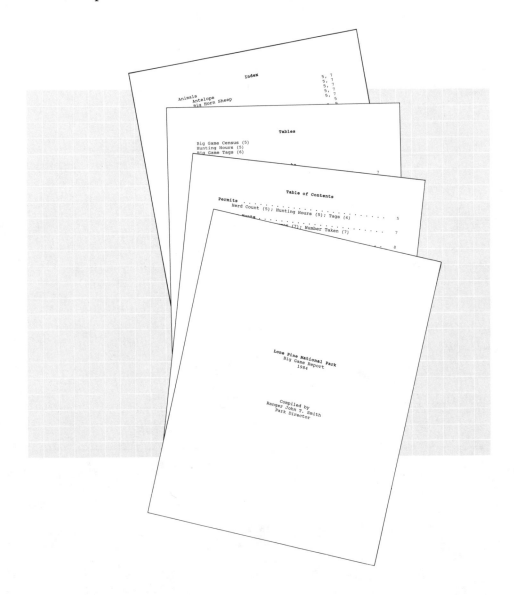

Index

Animals
   Antelope 5, 7
   Big Horn Sheep 5, 7

Tables

Big Game Census (5)
Hunting Hours (5)
Big Game Tags (6)

Table of Contents

Permits . . . .
   Herd Count (5); Hunting Hours (5); Tags (6) 5
Hunts . . . .
   . . . (7); Number Taken (7) 7

Lone Pine National Park
Big Game Report
1984

Compiled by
Ranger John T. Smith
Park Director

Concordance

If a document or report you are writing includes phrases which are repeated throughout the document, you can create a concordance file. Then, when you generate an index for the document, WordPerfect will search the document for every phrase listed in the concordance file. These entries will all be included in the index, along with the other words you specifically marked for the index in the document.

This lesson guides you through the basic steps of creating a concordance file. You retrieve a document, define an index style, and generate the index based on the phrases in the concordance.

While working through this lesson, you learn the following facts about WordPerfect's Concordance feature:

- The Concordance file is a regular WordPerfect document.
- Creating a Concordance file saves you the time it would take to individually mark each occurrence of the phrases in your document.
- Each phrase in the file must be separated by a Hard Return code [HRt].
- Each phrase in the file may have one or more associated index marks.
- Associated index marks must be placed before the Hard Return code.
- For multiple index marks associated with a given phrase, multiple index entries will be generated.
- Index generation is faster if your concordance entries are sorted alphabetically.

The skills you learn in this lesson can be used to

- Create a concordance file.
- Use a concordance file to help create an index.

18.1 Create a concordance file

Your concordance file will contain the names of the animals listed in the Lone Pine Big Game Report.

 , N , N   Clear the screen.

TYPE   **Deer**[HRt]
       Elk[HRt]
       Buffalo[HRt]
       Big Horn Sheep[HRt]
       Antelope[HRt]
       Rocky Mountain Goat[HRt]

Press the Enter key when you see [HRt].

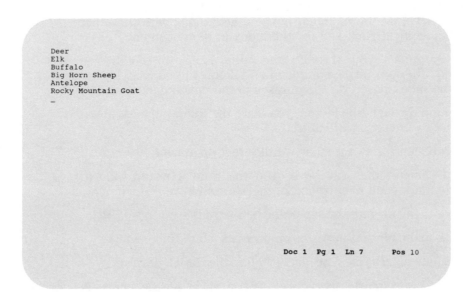

```
Deer
Elk
Buffalo
Big Horn Sheep
Antelope
Rocky Mountain Goat
_
```

                                                          Doc 1 Pg 1 Ln 7   Pos 10

18.2 Sort the names alphabetically

The index for your document generates faster if your concordance entries are sorted alphabetically.

Ctrl F9 , 2   Select the *Sort* option on the Merge/Sort menu.

↵   Accept the option of sorting the file on the screen.

↵   Accept the option of sorting to the screen.

The Sort menu appears on the bottom half of the screen. If "Sort by Line" is not the sort menu heading, press **7** for "Type" and **2** for "Line."

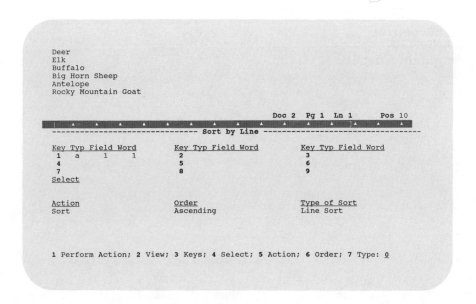

```
Deer
Elk
Buffalo
Big Horn Sheep
Antelope
Rocky Mountain Goat


                                       Doc 2  Pg 1  Ln 1      Pos 10

-------------------------------- Sort by Line ------------------------------------

Key Typ Field Word      Key Typ Field Word      Key Typ Field Word
  1   a    1    1          2                       3
  4                        5                       6
  7                        8                       9
Select


Action                  Order                   Type of Sort
Sort                    Ascending               Line Sort



1 Perform Action; 2 View; 3 Keys; 4 Select; 5 Action; 6 Order; 7 Type: 0
```

Because the default setting is to sort phrases alphabetically by the first word, you are ready to sort.

1 Select the *Perform Action* option to begin sorting.

18.3   Save the file

Save the concordance file in case of a power failure.

F10 Display the "Document to be Saved" message.

concord as the filename.

The concordance file is saved on disk and also remains on your screen.

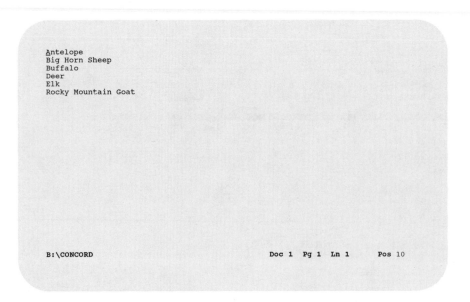

18.4 Insert index marks

The index marks associated with each concordance phrase will tell WordPerfect how to list the phrase in the index. Mark each phrase as a subheading for the index heading, "Animals."

[Alt] [F5] Display the Mark Text menu.

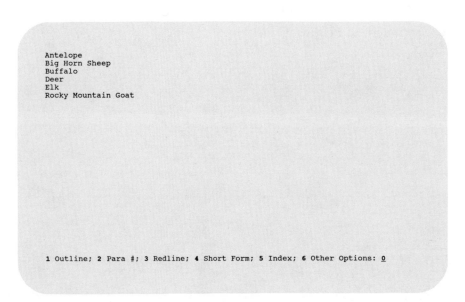

| 5 | Select the *Index* option. |

ENTER **Animals** for the heading.

```
Antelope
Big Horn Sheep
Buffalo
Deer
Elk
Rocky Mountain Goat








Subheading: Antelope
```

| ↵ | Accept "Antelope" for the subheading. |

| ↓ | Move the cursor to the second phrase in the file. |

| Alt F4 | Turn on Block. |

| End | Block the phrase. |

| Alt F5 , 5 | Select the *Index* option from the Mark Text menu. |

ENTER **Animals** for the heading.

| ↵ | Accept "Big Horn Sheep" for the subheading. |

| Home , ← | Return the cursor to the beginning of the line. |

| ↓ | Move the cursor to the next phrase in the file. |

Repeat these steps to mark the rest of the phrases. Remember to block the phrase if it includes more than one word.

18.5 Insert more index marks

For each of the animals, you also want to include another index mark which will list them individually in the index.

| Home , Home , ↑ | Move the cursor to the top line of the concordance file. |

| Alt F5 , 5 | Select the *Index* option from the Mark Text menu. |

```
Antelope
Big Horn Sheep
Buffalo
Deer
Elk
Rocky Mountain Goat
```



```
Index Heading: Antelope
```

⏎   Accept "Antelope" as the heading.

⏎   Do not include a subheading.

↓   Move the cursor to the second phrase in the file.

Alt F4   Turn on Block.

End   Block the phrase.

Alt F5 , 5   Select the *Index* option from the Mark Text menu.

⏎   Accept "Big Horn Sheep" as the heading.

⏎   Do not include a subheading.

Home , ←   Return the cursor to the beginning of the line.

↓   Move the cursor to the next phrase in the file.

Repeat these steps to mark the rest of the phrases. Remember to block the phrase if it includes more than one word.

Alt F3   Display the Reveal Codes screen to check that the index marks are to the left of the Hard Return codes [HRt] on each line.

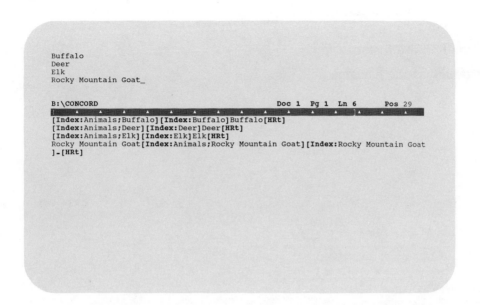

Space Bar   Exit the Reveal Codes screen.

18.6   Save the file again and clear the screen

You are ready to save the completed concordance file prior to using it in an index.

F7 , Y   Select the Save Document feature.

WordPerfect displays the CONCORD filename.

↵   Accept CONCORD as the filename.

Y   Accept the file on your screen as a replacement of the earlier file on disk.

↵   Clear the screen.

18.7 | Retrieve a document

Retrieve the document you want to use with the concordance file to create an index.

Shift F10 Select the Retrieve feature.

ENTER **report84.lrn** as the filename.

```
                        Lone Pine National Park
                            Big Game Report
                                 1984




                              Compiled by
                          Ranger John T. Smith
                             Park Director
=================================================================
                                PREFACE

            This report is a summary of the year's activities,
       as well as goals for the Big Game Reserve of Lone Pine
       National Park for 1985.



=================================================================
                               Permits

B:\REPORT84.LRN                       Doc 1  Pg 1  Ln 1     Pos 10
```

18.8 | Define the Index Style

Before you can generate an index, you must first define it for WordPerfect.

 , **,**   Move the cursor to the end of the document.

Ctrl ↵ Insert a Hard Page break.

Shift F6 Turn on centering.

F6 Turn on Bold.

TYPE **Index** for the index heading.

F6 Turn off Bold.

↵ Press 2 times to end centering, return the cursor to the next line, and add a blank line.

<kbd>Alt</kbd> <kbd>F5</kbd> , <kbd>6</kbd> Select *Other Options* from the Mark Text menu.

<kbd>5</kbd> Select the *Define Index* option, and the message "Concordance Filename (Enter=none):" appears on the status line.

```
Other Mark Text Options

    1 - Define Paragraph/Outline Numbering

    2 - Define Table of Contents

    3 - Define List

    4 - Define Table of Authorities

    5 - Define Index

    6 - Remove all Redline Markings and all Strikeout text from document

    7 - Edit Table of Authorities Full Form

    8 - Generate Tables and Index



Selection: 5
Concordance Filename (Enter=none): _
```

ENTER **concord**

TYPE **5** for Flush Right Page Numbers with Leaders.

You are returned to your document.

18.9	Generate the Index

With the concordance file created and the index style defined, you are now ready to generate an index for the Lone Pine Big Game Report.

<kbd>Alt</kbd> <kbd>F5</kbd> , <kbd>6</kbd> Select *Other Options* from the Mark Text menu.

<key>8</key>, <key>Y</key> Begin generating the index.

WordPerfect's counter lets you follow the progress.

<key>PgDn</key> View the newly created index.

```
                most of its outstanding obligations.  However, the
                donated funds mentioned in the proposal are needed to
                complete the 1985-86 projects.


        ==================================================================
                                      Index
        Animals
                Antelope . . . . . . . . . . . . . . . . . . 3, 5
                Big Horn Sheep . . . . . . . . . . . . . . . 3, 5
                Buffalo  . . . . . . . . . . . . . . . . . . 3, 5
                Deer . . . . . . . . . . . . . . . . . . . . 3, 5
                Elk  . . . . . . . . . . . . . . . . . . . . 3, 5
                Rocky Mountain Goat  . . . . . . . . . . . . 3, 5
        Antelope . . . . . . . . . . . . . . . . . . . . . . 3, 5
        Big Horn Sheep . . . . . . . . . . . . . . . . . . . 3, 5
        Buffalo  . . . . . . . . . . . . . . . . . . . . . . 3, 5
        Deer . . . . . . . . . . . . . . . . . . . . . . . . 3, 5
        Elk  . . . . . . . . . . . . . . . . . . . . . . . . 3, 5
        Rocky Mountain Goat  . . . . . . . . . . . . . . . . 3, 5
        _


        B:\REPORT84.LRN                    Doc 1   Pg 8   Ln 16      Pos 15
```

Table of Authorities

The Table of Authorities feature lets you generate a list of citations for a legal brief, detailing the pages where citings of specific cases and statutes occur.

You can define up to sixteen sections—one for cases, one for statutes, one for regulations, etc. The authorities within each section are sorted alphanumerically by WordPerfect. Each section of the table may have a different format, if you wish.

In this lesson, you mark, define, and generate a table of authorities.

While working through the lesson, you learn the following facts about WordPerfect's Table of Authorities feature:

- The first occurrence of an authority is marked with the full form of the citation.

- Subsequent occurrences of the same authority are marked with the short form of the citation.

- The Extended Search feature lets you search for authorities in footnotes and endnotes as well as in the text.

- The short form can be an excerpt of the full form or a word or phrase of your own choosing.

- Each full form must have its own unique short form.

- WordPerfect ties the short form to its associated full form and places the appropriate page numbers beside the full form in the table when it is generated.

The skills you learn in this lesson can be used to mark, define, and generate a table of authorities for a document.

19.1 Retrieve a document

Retrieve the TABLE.LRN document onto a clear screen.

Shift F10 Select the Retrieve feature.

ENTER **table.lrn** as the filename.

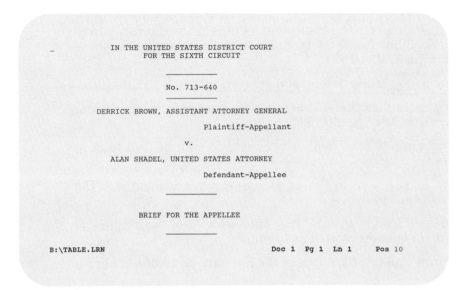

```
              IN THE UNITED STATES DISTRICT COURT
                    FOR THE SIXTH CIRCUIT

                          _____

                       No. 713-640
                          _____

   DERRICK BROWN, ASSISTANT ATTORNEY GENERAL

                          Plaintiff-Appellant

                       v.

   ALAN SHADEL, UNITED STATES ATTORNEY

                          Defendant-Appellee

                          _____

              BRIEF FOR THE APPELLEE
                          _____


B:\TABLE.LRN                          Doc 1  Pg 1  Ln 1    Pos 10
```

19.2 Mark with the full form

You are ready to mark the authorities that will be included in the table. Begin by marking the first occurrence of the Nelson case with the Full Form.

Home F2 Select the ▶Extended Search feature.

TYPE **nelson** as the search string.

F2 Begin the search. The cursor stops to the right of the word "Nelson."

Ctrl ← Move the cursor to the beginning of the name.

Alt F4 Turn on Block.

↓ Move down one line to block the entire case.

Alt F5 , 6 Select the *Table of Authorities* (ToA) option from the Mark Text menu.

ENTER **1** for the section number. You are placed in the special editing screen for authorities.

MOVE To the "M" at the beginning of the case number.

[↵] , [F4] Move the second half of the line below the first and indent it.

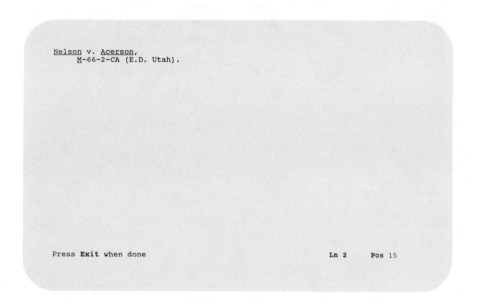

```
        Nelson v. Acerson,
             M-66-2-CA (E.D. Utah).




















Press Exit when done                              Ln 2      Pos 15
```

[F7] Save the changes and exit the editing screen.

<hr>

19.3   Selecting the short form

You need to select the short form to be associated with the full form you just marked. WordPerfect displays a default short form at the bottom of the screen (approximately 40 characters of the text blocked above).

MOVE To the space following "Nelson."

[Ctrl][End] Delete the remainder of the line.

[↵] Accept the edited short form.

[Alt][F3] Display the Reveal Codes screen to see the Table of Authorities code.

```
the Civil Rights Act of 1964 (31 U.S.C. § 1000e-15), and the

consent decree approved by this Court in Nelson v. Acerson, M-66-

2-CA (E.D. Utah).
--------------------------------------------------------------------------------
B:\TABLE.LRN                          Doc 1  Pg 1  Ln 46     Pos 51
▲    ▲    ▲    ▲    ▲    ▲    ▲    ▲    ▲    ▲    ▲    ▲     ▲    ▲
the Civil Rights Act of 1964 (31 U.S.C. § 1000e[-]15), and the[SRt]
consent decree approved by this Court in [ToA:1;Nelson;<Full Form>]_[U]Nelson[u]
 v. [U]Acerson[u], M[-]66[-]
2[-]CA (E.D. Utah).[SPg]
[TAB]Plaintiff also applied on May 4, 1984, for a temporary[SRt]
restraining order to prevent the defendant from carrying out the[SRt]
```

 Exit the Reveal Codes screen.

19.4   Mark with the short form

Continue marking all subsequent references to the Nelson case using the short form.

[End] Move past the first occurrence of the Nelson case.

[Home], [F2] Select the ▶Extended Search feature.

WordPerfect remembers and displays the search string you last used.

[F2] Begin the search. The cursor stops to the right of "Nelson" on the bottom of page 2.

`Alt` `F5` , `2`   Select the *Short Form* option from the Mark Text menu.

WordPerfect displays the default short form you last entered.

```
liberty interest since the agency never made nor is it likely to
make the allegedly stigmatizing charges public in any official or
intentional manner, other than in connection with the defense of
this action.  Finally, the undisputed facts in this case undercut
plaintiff's claims that his removal violated the First Amendment,
Title VII and/or the consent decree entered in the Nelson case;
indeed, the record evidence establishes that plaintiff's removal
had nothing to do with his advocacy of affirmative action for
-------------------------------------------------------------------
women and minorities, but rather was based upon a determination
by HHS's General Counsel that plaintiff could not be trusted to
carry out effectively the duties of an Assistant Attorney
General.2
Enter Short Form:  Nelson
```

`↵`   Accept the displayed short form.

Repeat the above steps until all occurrences of "Nelson" are marked for the Table of Authorities.

19.5   Mark another authority

Mark a statute which will be placed in section 2 of the Table of Authorities when the table is generated.

`Home` , `Home` , `↑`   Move to the beginning of the document.

Begin marking the Civil Rights Act.

`Home` , `F2`   Select the ▶Extended Search feature.

TYPE   **civil** as the search string.

| F2 | Begin the search. The cursor stops to the right of the word "Civil." |

| Ctrl ← | Move the cursor to the beginning of the word. |

| Alt F4 | Turn on Block. |

TYPE **)** (a right parenthesis) to block the statute.

```
     Regional Office effective May 5, 1984.  On May 4, 1984, plaintiff

     filed this action against then Secretary John Lewisl charging

     that HHS's decision to terminate his employment violated the

     First and Fifth Amendments to the United States Constitution, the

     Administrative Procedure Act (4 U.S.C. §§ 600-605), Title VII of

     the Civil Rights Act of 1964 (31 U.S.C. § 1000e-15), and the

     consent decree approved by this Court in Nelson v. Acerson, M-66-

     2-CA (E.D. Utah).
     --------------------------------------------------------------------
         Plaintiff also applied on May 4, 1984, for a temporary

     restraining order to prevent the defendant from carrying out the

     proposed termination.  The Court granted the requested

     restraining order on May 5, 1984.  However, on June 5, 1984,

  Block on                                   Doc 1  Pg 1  Ln 44    Pos 61
```

| Alt F5 , 6 | Select the *Table of Authorities* (ToA) option from the Mark Text menu. |

ENTER **2** for the section number. You are placed in the special editing screen for authorities.

No editing is required.

| F7 | Exit the editing screen. |

Define the short form.

MOVE To the space following "Act."

| Ctrl End | Delete the remainder of the line. |

| ↵ | Accept the edited short form. |

Because the Civil Rights Act is only referred to once in the brief, no short forms need to be marked.

19.6 | Mark a third authority

Mark another statute which will also be placed in section 2 of the Table of Authorities when the table is generated.

Home , Home , ↑   Move to the beginning of the document.

Begin marking the Administrative Procedure Act.

Home , F2   Select the ▶Extended Search feature.

TYPE   **Act** as the search string.   *Remember to capitalize the "A" in "Acts."*

F2   Begin the search. The cursor stops to the right of the word "Act" in the Administrative Procedure Act statute.

Ctrl ←   Press 3 times to move the cursor to the beginning of the word "Administrative."

Alt F4   Turn on Block.

TYPE   **)** (a right parenthesis) to block the statute.

Alt F5 , 6   Select the *Table of Authorities* (ToA) option from the Mark Text menu.

```
position as Assistant Attorney General for the Orem, Utah,
Regional Office effective May 5, 1984.  On May 4, 1984, plaintiff
filed this action against then Secretary John Lewis1 charging
that HHS's decision to terminate his employment violated the
First and Fifth Amendments to the United States Constitution, the
Administrative Procedure Act (4 U.S.C. §§ 600-605), Title VII of
the Civil Rights Act of 1964 (31 U.S.C. § 1000e-15), and the
consent decree approved by this Court in Nelson v. Acerson, M-66-
2-CA (E.D. Utah).
--------------------------------------------------------------------
     Plaintiff also applied on May 4, 1984, for a temporary
restraining order to prevent the defendant from carrying out the
proposed termination.  The Court granted the requested
ToA section number (Press Enter for short form only): _
```

ENTER   **2** for the section number. You are placed in the special editing screen for authorities.

No editing is required.

F7   Exit the editing screen.

Define the short form.

MOVE To the space following "Act."

<kbd>Ctrl</kbd> <kbd>End</kbd> Delete the remainder of the line.

<kbd>↵</kbd> Accept the edited short form.

Because the Administrative Procedure Act is only referred to once in the brief, no short forms need to be marked.

19.7 Define the first section

When you define sections, you specify the section in which you would like each authority listed. You can also choose dot leaders, underlining, or double spacing in each section.

<kbd>Home</kbd> , <kbd>Home</kbd> , <kbd>↑</kbd> Move to the top of the document.

<kbd>Ctrl</kbd> <kbd>↵</kbd> Insert a page break so the Table of Authorities will be separated from the rest of the text.

<kbd>↑</kbd> Move the cursor above the page break.

<kbd>Shift</kbd> <kbd>F6</kbd> Turn on centering.

TYPE **TABLE OF AUTHORITIES**

<kbd>↵</kbd> Press 3 times to return the cursor to the next line and add spacing after the title.

TYPE **CASES**

<kbd>Alt</kbd> <kbd>F6</kbd> Align text at the right margin.

TYPE **Page:**

<kbd>↵</kbd> Press 2 times to return the cursor to the next line and add a blank line.

```
                    TABLE OF AUTHORITIES

CASES                                                    Page:
_
================================================================================
             IN THE UNITED STATES DISTRICT COURT
                   FOR THE SIXTH CIRCUIT
                        _____

                        No. 713-640
                        _____

        DERRICK BROWN, ASSISTANT ATTORNEY GENERAL

                          Plaintiff-Appellant

                    v.

        ALAN SHADEL, UNITED STATES ATTORNEY

                          Defendant-Appellee

B:\TABLE.LRN                        Doc 1  Pg 1  Ln 6      Pos 10
```

Alt F5 , 6 Select *Other Options* from the Mark Text menu.

4 Select the *Define Table of Authorities* option.

ENTER 1 to define section 1.

TYPE 1 for Dot leaders.

Y Confirm dot leaders for section 1.

⏎ Save the format and exit to the document.

19.8 Define the second section

You are ready to define the second section of the Table of Authorities.

TYPE STATUTES

⏎ Press 2 times to return the cursor to the next line and add a blank line.

[Alt] [F5] , [6] Select *Other Options* from the Mark Text menu.

[4] Select the *Define Table of Authorities* option.

ENTER **2** to define section 2.

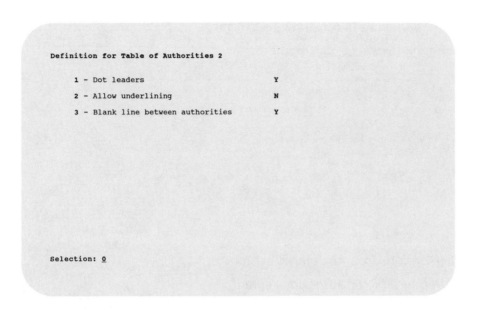

```
Definition for Table of Authorities 2

    1 - Dot leaders                        Y

    2 - Allow underlining                  N

    3 - Blank line between authorities     Y









Selection: 0
```

TYPE **1** for Dot leaders.

[N] Do not put dot leaders in section 2.

TYPE **3** for Blank line between authorities.

[N] Do not put a blank line between authorities.

[↵] Save the format and exit to the document.

[↓] Move to the first line of page 2.

Page numbers must be set for the document beginning on the page after the Table of Authorities in order for the table to generate accurately.

[Home] , [Home] , [Home] , [←] Move to the beginning of the line before any codes.

[Alt] [F8] , [2] Select the *New Page Number* option on the Page Format menu to specify a new page number.

ENTER **1** for the new page number.

TYPE **1** to select Arabic style page numbers.

[↵] Exit the Page Format menu.

19.9 Generate the Table of Authorities

With each citation marked for the Table of Authorities, you are ready to generate. You may begin generation from anywhere in the document.

`Alt` `F5` , `6`   Select *Other Options* from the Mark Text menu.

`8` , `Y`   Begin generating the Table of Authorities.

WordPerfect's counter lets you follow the progress.

```
                    TABLE OF AUTHORITIES


        CASES                                        Page:

        Nelson v. Acerson,
           M-66-2-CA (E.D. Utah).  . . . . . . . . . . . . . . . 1-4

        STATUTES

        Administrative Procedure Act (4 U.S.C. §§ 600-605)      1
        Civil Rights Act of 1964 (31 U.S.C. § 1000e-15)         1


        ===================================================================
                      IN THE UNITED STATES DISTRICT COURT
                            FOR THE SIXTH CIRCUIT

                            _____

                            No. 713-640
                            _____

               DERRICK BROWN, ASSISTANT ATTORNEY GENERAL

        B:\TABLE.LRN                    Doc 1  Pg 1  Ln 11    Pos 10
```

19.10 Print and save the document

Print and save the legal brief with its Table of Authorities.

`Shift` `F7` , `1`   Select the *Full Text* option on the Print menu to print the document.

`F7` , `Y`   Begin saving the document.

`End`   Move to the end of the filename.

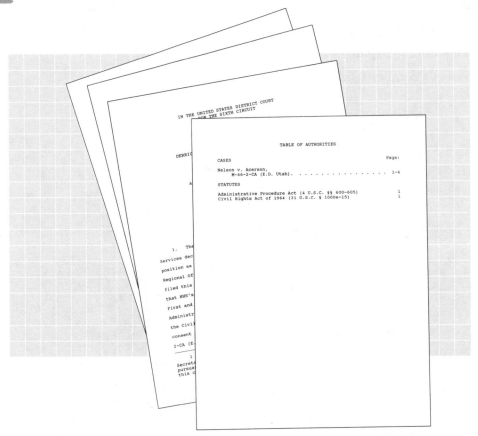

Press 3 times to delete "lrn."

ENTER **1** to name the file **table.1**.

Clear the screen.

IN THE UNITED STATES DISTRICT COURT
FOR THE SIXTH CIRCUIT

DERRIC

A

1.   The
Services dec
position as
Regional Of
filed this
that HHS's
First and
Administr
the Civil
consent
2-CA (E-

1
Secreta
pursua
this c

TABLE OF AUTHORITIES

CASES   Page:

Nelson v. Acerson,
    M-66-2-CA (E.D. Utah).   1-4

STATUTES

Administrative Procedure Act (4 U.S.C. §§ 600-605)   1
Civil Rights Act of 1964 (31 U.S.C. § 1000e-15)   1

Line Draw

The Line Draw feature helps you draw boxes, graphs, borders, and other illustrations using DOS graphics characters (or any DOS character). The quality of the printed copy depends on your printer's character set.

In this lesson, you use the Line Draw feature to draw a box around the title of the Lone Pine Big Game report, then print the title page.

While working through the lesson, you learn the following facts about WordPerfect's Line Draw feature:

- You can draw on a clear screen, or around and over existing text.

- If you are drawing a box, corners are inserted automatically as you change directions.

- Blank areas are filled in with spaces and/or Hard Returns to help create the illustration.

- The *Move* option on the Line Draw menu lets you move around the illustration without disturbing any characters.

- Using the Arrow keys inserts the graphics character.

The skills you learn in this lesson can be used to draw boxes, graphs, borders, and other illustrations.

Line Draw operates in the Typeover mode. When the cursor passes through existing characters, they are replaced. Codes are pushed forward.

20.1   Retrieve a document

Retrieve the Big Game report for editing.

Shift F10 Select the Retrieve feature.

ENTER **report84.lrn** as the filename.

```
                    Lone Pine National Park
                        Big Game Report
                             1984




                         Compiled by
                     Ranger John T. Smith
                        Park Director
=================================================================
                          PREFACE
         This report is a summary of the year's activities,
       as well as goals for the Big Game Reserve of Lone Pine
       National Park for 1985.



=================================================================
                          Permits

B:\REPORT84.LRN                    Doc 1  Pg 1  Ln 1      Pos 10
```

20.2 Double space the title

The text for the title is in three centered lines. Extra space is needed above the text, and the text would look better if double spaced.

→ Move past the Center Page code.

↵ Press 2 times to add blank lines.

↓ , ← Move to the beginning of the "Big Game Report" line.

↵ Add a blank line.

⬇ , ⬅   Move to the beginning of the "1984" line.

↵   Add a blank line.

```
              Lone Pine National Park

                 Big Game Report

                      1984




                    Compiled by
                Ranger John T. Smith
                   Park Director
=============================================================================
                       PREFACE
            This report is a summary of the year's activities,
         as well as goals for the Big Game Reserve of Lone Pine
         National Park for 1985.



   B:\REPORT84.LRN                        Doc 1  Pg 1  Ln 7     Pos 10
```

20.3   Draw the box

You are ready to use the Line Draw feature to draw a rectangular box around the text.

Ctrl F3 , 2   Select the *Line Draw* option on the Screen menu. The Line Draw menu appears.

6   Select the *Move* option.

MOVE   To Line 1 Position 26.

Use the Arrow keys to move the cursor. When this document was created, no spaces were inserted into the empty lines; however, when you use Line Draw, WordPerfect inserts spaces into the empty lines to help move the cursor where you want it.

1   Begin drawing with a single line character "|".

MOVE   To Line 1 Position 58.

As you move the cursor, the single line graphics character is inserted for you. Once you reach the spot where you want to form a right angle, you are ready to draw the right side of the box.

MOVE   To Line 8 Position 58.

Notice how WordPerfect continues to add spaces as they are needed to create the box.

Esc , 3 , 2	Set the Escape value for 32 times.
←	Draw a single line 32 characters long.

You can use the Escape feature to repeat a character as many times as you wish.

The line is too close to the text, and needs to be erased and moved down.

5	Select the *Erase* option.
MOVE	To Line 8 Position 58 to erase the line.
1	Begin drawing with a single line character.
↓	Add an extra line for spacing.
Esc , 3 , 2	Set the Escape value for 32 times.
←	Redraw the line.
Esc , ↑	Finish drawing the box.

Now that the box is complete, you are ready to exit the Line Draw menu and print the edited title page.

F7	Exit the Line Draw menu.

```
          ┌─────────────────────────┐
          │ Lone Pine National Park │
          │                         │
          │    Big Game Report      │
          │                         │
          │         1984            │
          └─────────────────────────┘




                    Compiled by
                 Ranger John T. Smith
                   Park Director
================================================================================
                      PREFACE
          This report is a summary of the year's activities,
        as well as goals for the Big Game Reserve of Lone Pine
        National Park for 1985.


  B:\REPORT84.LRN                    Doc 1  Pg 1  Ln 1      Pos 26
```

Print a page

Your printer may not be able to reproduce the graphics characters you have used to draw the box. Follow the steps below to send the page to the printer as a test.

Shift F7 , 2   Select the *Page* option on the Print menu to print the edited title page.

F7 , N , ↵   Clear the screen.

Lone Pine National Park

Big Game Report

1984

Compiled by
Ranger John T. Smith
Park Director

Lesson 21

Macro Chaining

The Macro feature lets you record any keystrokes, both text and function keys, under one name, and play them back exactly as they were recorded. Any task you perform repeatedly is a candidate for the Macro feature.

Macro chaining involves linking two or more macros together so that when one finishes, the other will automatically start.

In this lesson, you create a simple macro chain that marks a phrase for indexing, then moves on to the next page where the phrase occurs.

While working through the lesson, you learn the following facts about WordPerfect's Macro feature:

- When you chain two macros together in a simple chain, all the keystrokes in the first macro are completed before WordPerfect starts the second macro.

- When you insert a search into a macro, the search is actually performed while you are recording the macro.

The skills you learn in this lesson can be used to quickly and accurately perform a task which you need to perform repeatedly throughout a document.

21.1　Retrieve a document

Retrieve the Big Game report onto a clear screen.

 Select the Retrieve feature.

ENTER **report84.lrn** as the filename.

```
                    Lone Pine National Park
                       Big Game Report
                           1984




                         Compiled by
                     Ranger John T. Smith
                       Park Director
==================================================================
                           PREFACE

           This report is a summary of the year's activities,
         as well as goals for the Big Game Reserve of Lone Pine
         National Park for 1985.



     ==================================================================
                           Permits

  B:\REPORT84.LRN                       Doc 1  Pg 1  Ln 1      Pos 10
```

Create the SEARCH macro

In this step, you create a macro that moves down one page, then searches for the phrase "Big Game Permits."

Ctrl F10 Select the Macro Define feature to begin defining the SEARCH macro.

ENTER **search** as the macro name.

PgDn Move to the top of the next page.

F2 Select the ◆Search feature.

TYPE **Big Game Permits** as the search string.

F2 Begin the search. The cursor stops just to the right of the first occurrence of "Big Game Permits."

Ctrl F10 Select the Macro Define feature to end defining the macro.

```
              Big Horn Sheep. . . . . .7 a.m. to 4 p.m.
              Buffalo. . . . . . . . . 12 p.m. to dusk
              Deer. . . . . . . . . . .daylight hours
              Elk. . . . . . . . . . . 8 a.m. to dusk
              Rocky Mountain Goat. . . 12 p.m. to 12:01 p.m.



==================================================================
         Tags

         The Big Game Permits_were issued by lottery, bid, and
         once-in-a-lifetime priorities.  All permits were
         monitored by the Checking Stations during the 1984
         hunts.

             1.    Tags were removed by the Checking Stations and
                   returned to the Ranger Station Headquarters.

             2.    Any permits not accounted by receipt of tags
                   were contacted by mail through Ranger Station
                   Headquarters.

         The following table reflects the average number of

B:\REPORT84.LRN                    Doc 1  Pg 4  Ln 3      Pos 35
```

21.3 Create the ALT-I macro

You are now ready to create an ALT-I macro that inserts an Index code for a "Big Game Permits" heading, then starts the Search macro to find the next occurrence of "Big Game Permits."

Ctrl F10 Select the Macro Define feature to begin defining the ALT-I macro.

Alt I Name the macro using the Alt key.

Alt F10 Select the Macro feature to start the SEARCH macro.

ENTER **search** as the macro name.

You have just chained the SEARCH macro to the ALT-I macro. However, the SEARCH macro will not start until you start the ALT-I macro in the last step of this lesson.

Alt F5 , 5 Select the *Index* option on the Mark Text menu to display the "Index Heading:" message.

ENTER **Big Game Permits** for the heading.

Space Bar , Back-space , ↵ Erase the displayed subheading and insert the Index code.

Ctrl F10 Select the Macro Define feature to end defining the ALT-I macro.

[Backspace] , [Y]   Delete the Index code.

[Home] , [Home] , [↑]   Return to the beginning of the report.

21.4 Start the ALT-I macro

You are ready to use the chained macros on the Big Game report.

[Alt] [I]   Start the ALT-I macro.

The ALT-I macro marks "Big Game Permits" then starts the SEARCH macro. This macro moves the cursor to the next page and searches for the next occurrence of the phrase. If you want to mark that next occurrence of "Big Game Permits," start the ALT-I macro again; otherwise, do a forward search for the next occurrence.

```
          Big Horn Sheep. . . . . .7 a.m. to 4 p.m.
          Buffalo. . . . . . . . . 12 p.m. to dusk
          Deer. . . . . . . . . . .daylight hours
          Elk. . . . . . . . . . . 8 a.m. to dusk
          Rocky Mountain Goat. . . 12 p.m. to 12:01 p.m.



    =================================================================
        Tags

        The Big Game Permits_were issued by lottery, bid, and
        once-in-a-lifetime priorities.  All permits were
        monitored by the Checking Stations during the 1984
        hunts.

             1.   Tags were removed by the Checking Stations and
                  returned to the Ranger Station Headquarters.

             2.   Any permits not accounted by receipt of tags
                  were contacted by mail through Ranger Station
                  Headquarters.

        The following table reflects the average number of

    B:\REPORT84.LRN                     Doc 1  Pg 4  Ln 3      Pos 35
```

Lesson 22

Repeating Macro Chains

When you are searching through a document, you usually want to find every occurrence of the search string. You can create a macro that will perform a search, then chain that macro to itself so it searches over and over for the search string. The macro ends when the search results in a "* Not Found *". This kind of macro chain is called a repeating chain.

In this lesson, you create a macro that marks every occurrence of a phrase for indexing.

While working through the lesson, you learn the following facts about WordPerfect's Macro feature:

• Repeating chains are especially useful when searching through your document for a recurring phrase.

• A repeating chain is created when you link a macro to itself.

The skills you learn in this lesson can be used to quickly and accurately perform a task which you need to perform repeatedly throughout a document.

 22.1 **Retrieve a document**

Retrieve the Big Game report onto a clear screen.

Shift F10   Select the Retrieve feature.

ENTER **report84.lrn** as the filename.

```
                    Lone Pine National Park
                       Big Game Report
                           1984




                        Compiled by
                   Ranger John T. Smith
                      Park Director
=================================================================
                         PREFACE

          This report is a summary of the year's activities,
        as well as goals for the Big Game Reserve of Lone Pine
        National Park for 1985.



=================================================================
                        Permits

B:\REPORT84.LRN                      Doc 1  Pg 1  Ln 1    Pos 10
```

22.2   Create the INDEX macro

In this step, you create a repeating macro that marks every occurrence of "Big Game Permits" in the report. Because there is a ♦Search in the macro, the macro automatically stops when WordPerfect cannot find the phrase.

Ctrl F10 Select the Macro Define feature to begin defining the INDEX macro.

ENTER **index** as the macro name.

F2 Select the ♦Search feature.

TYPE **Big Game Permits** for the search string.

F2 Begin the search.

Alt F5 , 5 Select the *Index* option on the Mark Text menu to display the "Index Heading:" message.

ENTER **Big Game Permits** for the heading.

Space Bar , Back-space , ↵ Erase the displayed subheading and insert the Index code.

22.3   Chain the macro to itself

You are now ready to create a repeating macro by chaining the INDEX macro to itself.

Alt F10 Select the Macro feature to start the macro.

ENTER **index** as the macro name.

Ctrl F10 Select the Macro Define feature to end defining the INDEX macro.

Back-space , Y Delete the Index code.

Home , Home , ↑ Return to the beginning of the report.

22.4 Start the INDEX macro

With the cursor at the beginning of the document, you are ready to start the repeating macro.

Alt F10 Select the Macro feature to start the macro.

ENTER **index** as the macro name.

When every occurrence of "Big Game Permits" has been found and marked, the macro stops at the end of the report.

```
        Heights").

            The goals and improvements for the 1985-86 hunts
        are given in detail in the Program Improvements Report.



        ===============================================================================
                                        Summary

            Because of increased revenues during 1984, due
        largely to Big Game Permits, the park was able to meet
        most of its outstanding obligations.  However, the
        donated funds mentioned in the proposal are needed to
        complete the 1985-86 projects.




B:\REPORT84.LRN                              Doc 1  Pg 7  Ln 4      Pos 42
```

Conditional Macro Chains

A conditional macro chain will perform a search, then *make a decision*, depending on the search findings. You create a conditional chain by starting two macros while defining a "Search" macro. One is a "Found" macro (completed if the "Search" macro is successful) and the other is a "Not Found" macro (completed if the "Search" macro is unsuccessful).

In this lesson, you create a macro that stops at a phrase and lets you enter the heading and subheading for indexing. If the phrase is not found, you are returned to the beginning of the report.

While working through the lesson, you learn the following facts about WordPerfect's Macro feature:

- When you start a "Search" macro, it will chain to either the "Found" or the "Not Found" macro, depending on the success or failure of the search.

- The "Search" macro must include the keystrokes for a search.

The skills you learn in this lesson can be used to quickly and accurately perform either one of two tasks, depending on the outcome of a search.

23.1 | Retrieve a document

Retrieve the Big Game report onto a clear screen.

 Select the Retrieve feature.

ENTER **report84.lrn** as the filename.

```
                    Lone Pine National Park
                       Big Game Report
                           1984




                          Compiled by
                     Ranger John T. Smith
                        Park Director
==============================================================================
                           PREFACE

            This report is a summary of the year's activities,
          as well as goals for the Big Game Reserve of Lone Pine
          National Park for 1985.



==============================================================================
                           Permits

   B:\REPORT84.LRN                          Doc 1  Pg 1  Ln 1    Pos 10
```

23.2 Create the MARK macro

A conditional chain involves three types of macros: "Found," "Not Found," and "Search." In this step, you create the "Found" macro for the chain. This macro selects the Index marking feature.

Ctrl F10 Select the Macro Define feature to begin defining the MARK macro.

ENTER **mark** as the macro name.

Alt F5 , 5 Select the *Index* option on the Mark Text menu. Do not enter a heading or subheading.

Ctrl F10 Select the Macro Define feature to end defining the MARK macro. The "Index Heading:" message still appears on the screen.

```
                    Lone Pine National Park
                       Big Game Report
                           1984




                         Compiled by
                     Ranger John T. Smith
                        Park Director
==========================================================================
                           PREFACE
            This report is a summary of the year's activities,
        as well as goals for the Big Game Reserve of Lone Pine
        National Park for 1985.


==========================================================================
                           Permits

Index Heading:  _
```

F1 Cancel the Index feature.

23.3   Create the BEGIN macro

In this step, you create the "Not Found" macro. This macro returns the cursor to the beginning of the report.

Ctrl F10 Select the Macro Define feature to begin defining the BEGIN macro.

ENTER **begin** as the macro name.

Home , Home , ↑ Return to the beginning of the report.

Ctrl F10 Select the Macro Define feature to end defining the BEGIN macro.

23.4   Create the ALT-S macro

You are ready to create the "Search" macro for the repeating chain. This macro links all three types together.

Ctrl F10 Select the Macro Define feature to begin defining the ALT-S macro.

Alt S Name the macro with the Alt key.

Alt F10 Select the Macro feature to start the BEGIN macro.

ENTER **begin** as the macro name.

F2 Select the ♦Search feature.

TYPE **Big Game Permits** as the search string.

F2 Begin the search.

```
                Big Horn Sheep. . . . . .7 a.m. to 4 p.m.
                Buffalo. . . . . . . . . 12 p.m. to dusk
                Deer. . . . . . . . . . .daylight hours
                Elk. . . . . . . . . . 8 a.m. to dusk
                Rocky Mountain Goat. . . 12 p.m. to 12:01 p.m.


        ----------------------------------------------------------------------
        Tags

        The Big Game Permits_were issued by lottery, bid, and
        once-in-a-lifetime priorities.  All permits were
        monitored by the Checking Stations during the 1984
        hunts.

            1.    Tags were removed by the Checking Stations and
                  returned to the Ranger Station Headquarters.

            2.    Any permits not accounted by receipt of tags
                  were contacted by mail through Ranger Station
                  Headquarters.

            The following table reflects the average number of

        Macro Def                          Doc 1  Pg 4  Ln 3     Pos 35
```

Alt F10 Select the Macro feature to start the MARK macro.

ENTER **mark** as the macro name.

Ctrl F10 Select the Macro Define feature to end defining the ALT-S macro.

Home , Home , ↑ Return the cursor to the beginning of the report.

23.5 Start the ALT-S macro

You are now ready to start using the "Search" macro (ALT-S). The macro searches for the phrase "Big Game Reports." If the phrase is found, WordPerfect starts the MARK macro; if the phrase is not found, WordPerfect starts the BEGIN macro.

Alt S Start the ALT-S macro.

The macro stops to let you enter the heading and subheading. After entering the text, start the conditional macro again by pressing ALT-S. When the phrase is no longer found, you are returned to the beginning of the report.

```
    ─                    Lone Pine National Park
                              Big Game Report
                                   1984




                                 Compiled by
                             Ranger John T. Smith
                                Park Director
    ===================================================================
                                   PREFACE

                  This report is a summary of the year's activities,
              as well as goals for the Big Game Reserve of Lone Pine
              National Park for 1985.



    ===================================================================
                                   Permits

    B:\REPORT84.LRN                         Doc 1  Pg 1  Ln 1     Pos 10
```

Lesson 24

 ## Repeating Conditional Macro Chains

The repeating conditional chain is very similar to the conditional chain. The only difference is that in the repeating chain, the Search macro is chained to itself, and then chained to a "Not Found" macro. The macro repeats itself over and over until the search string is no longer found, then starts the "Not Found" macro.

In this lesson, you create a macro that stops at *every occurrence* of a phrase and marks it for indexing. When the phrase is no longer found, you are returned to the beginning of the report.

While working through the lesson, you learn the following facts about WordPerfect's features:

- The "Not Found" macro should be started at the beginning of the "Search" macro.

- The "Search" macro should be chained to itself at the end of the "Search" macro.

The skills you learn in this lesson can be used to quickly and accurately perform either of two tasks, depending on the outcome of a search.

24.1 | Retrieve a document

Retrieve the Big Game report onto a clear screen.

 Shift F10   Select the Retrieve feature.

ENTER   **report84.lrn** as the filename.

```
                        Lone Pine National Park
                           Big Game Report
                               1984




                              Compiled by
                          Ranger John T. Smith
                             Park Director
============================================================================
                               PREFACE
              This report is a summary of the year's activities,
         as well as goals for the Big Game Reserve of Lone Pine
         National Park for 1985.



============================================================================
                               Permits

B:\REPORT84.LRN                          Doc 1  Pg 1  Ln 1      Pos 10
```

24.2 | Create the BEGIN macro

This is the "Not Found" macro that returns the cursor to the beginning of the report.

If you have not already done so, create the BEGIN macro described in Lesson 23.

24.3 | Create the PERMIT macro

In this step, you create the "Search" macro. Then, you create a repeating conditional macro by chaining the PERMIT macro to the BEGIN macro and back to itself again.

Ctrl F10 Select the Macro Define feature to begin defining the PERMIT macro.

ENTER **permit** as the macro name.

Alt F10 Select the Macro feature to start the BEGIN macro.

ENTER **begin** as the macro name.

F2 Select the ▶Search feature.

TYPE **Big Game Permits** as the search string.

F2 Begin the search.

Alt F5 , 5 Select the *Index* option on the Mark Text menu to display the "Index Heading:" message.

ENTER **Big Game Permits** as the heading.

Keys	Description
Space Bar , Back-space , ↵	Erase the displayed subheading and insert the Index code.
Alt F10	Select the Macro feature to start the PERMIT macro.
ENTER	**permit** as the macro name.
Ctrl F10	Select the Macro Define feature to end defining the PERMIT macro.
Back-space , Y	Delete the Index code.

24.4 Start the PERMIT macro

You are now ready to start using the PERMIT macro. The macro marks every occurrence of "Big Game Permits" for an index. When the phrase is no longer found, WordPerfect starts the BEGIN macro and returns you to the beginning of the report.

Keys	Description
Home , Home , ↑	Move to the beginning of the report.
Alt F10	Select the Macro feature to start the PERMIT macro.
ENTER	**permit** as the macro name.

```
                        Lone Pine National Park
                            Big Game Report
                                 1984




                              Compiled by
                          Ranger John T. Smith
                            Park Director
================================================================================
                                PREFACE

           This report is a summary of the year's activities,
        as well as goals for the Big Game Reserve of Lone Pine
        National Park for 1985.



================================================================================
                                Permits

B:\REPORT84.LRN                              Doc 1  Pg 1  Ln 1      Pos 10
```

Line Sort

WordPerfect's Sort feature can look at single lines of text and sort them according to your directions. In this lesson, you do a line sort by last and first names. Since field 1 has an irregular number of words, you must count from right to left to identify the exact location of the surname.

While working through the lesson, you learn the following facts about WordPerfect's Sort feature:

- Lines end with Hard Returns [HRt].

- Fields in a line sort are divided by tabs and indents.

- Words in a field are separated by spaces.

- A document can be sorted from the screen.

- A document can be sorted to the screen.

- When defining keys, use the Arrow keys to move within a key and the Enter key to move to the next key.

- Negative numbers can be used to count from right to left in a field.

The skills you learn in this lesson can be used for organizing and arranging lists of any kind.

25.1 Retrieve a document

Retrieve a passenger list onto the screen and prepare to sort it. Start with a clear screen.

 Select the Retrieve feature.

ENTER **passage.4** as the filename.

```
Henry J. Cahoon        Belgium    786-5632  TWA        1st C
Robert R. Thompson     Holland    912-3356  United     coach
Gerald Jensen          Orlando    382-4391  Western    1st C
Patricia Pace          Redding    821-2119  United     coach
Tom Fielding           Phoenix    798-5233  TWA        coach
Steven M. Gentry       Columbus   734-8970  Republic   coach
Doug Gerrard           New York   553-8571  KLM        1st C
Ted Clegg              Vegas      244-1730  Delta      coach
Sherry Anderson        Boston     322-3161  Eastern    coach
Don Bassett            England    225-7338  TWA        1st C
Carl J. Fields         Sweden     255-1076  TWA        coach
Mary C. Hyde           Maine      225-1555  Frontier   coach
Ronald Jacobs          New York   373-2248  TWA        1st C
Patty Little           Portland   244-2676  Western    coach
Cathy White            LA         433-6713  Western    coach
Fred Collins           Calif      553-4981  Republic   coach
Daniel Jacobs          LA         322-7502  Western    coach
Scott J. Larsen        Calif      244-3566  Western    coach
Ted H. Pryor           New York   255-2954  TWA        coach
Conrad Silvers         D.C.       734-9132  TWA        coach
Helen Curtis           LA         373-2604  Western    1st C
Ken Anderson           New York   433-1831  TWA        coach



B:\PASSAGE.◄                              Doc 1  Pg 1  Ln 1     Pos 10
```

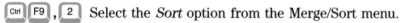 **Ctrl F9** , **2** Select the *Sort* option from the Merge/Sort menu.

↵ Accept the option of sorting the file on the screen.

↵ Accept the option of sorting to the screen. The Sort menu appears on the bottom half of the screen. If "Sort by Line" is not the Sort menu heading, press **7** for "Type" and **2** for "Line."

25.2 Define keys

Define two keys to sort the passengers alphabetically by last and first name.

3 Select the *Keys* option to define keys 1 and 2.

As you define keys, use the Right and Left Arrow keys to move from entry to entry.

ENTER **a 1 -1** for key1.

ENTER **a 1 1** for key2.

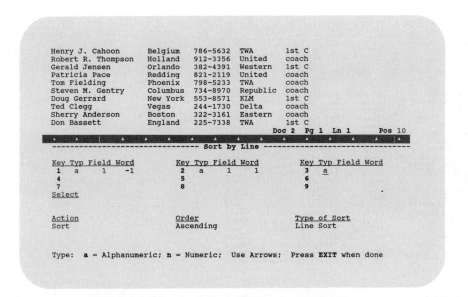

F7   Exit to the Sort menu.

You are now ready to sort the PASSAGE.4 file.

1 Select the *Perform Action* option to begin sorting.

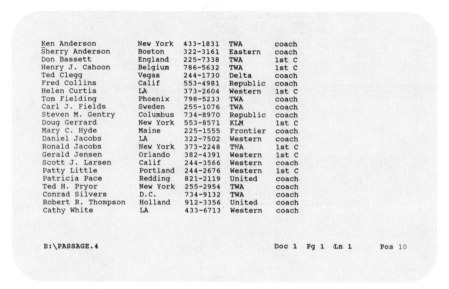

```
Ken Anderson        New York   433-1831   TWA        coach
Sherry Anderson     Boston     322-3161   Eastern    coach
Don Bassett         England    225-7338   TWA        1st C
Henry J. Cahoon     Belgium    786-5632   TWA        1st C
Ted Clegg           Vegas      244-1730   Delta      coach
Fred Collins        Calif      553-4981   Republic   coach
Helen Curtis        LA         373-2604   Western    1st C
Tom Fielding        Phoenix    798-5233   TWA        coach
Carl J. Fields      Sweden     255-1076   TWA        coach
Steven M. Gentry    Columbus   734-8970   Republic   coach
Doug Gerrard        New York   553-8571   KLM        1st C
Mary C. Hyde        Maine      225-1555   Frontier   coach
Daniel Jacobs       LA         322-7502   Western    coach
Ronald Jacobs       New York   373-2248   TWA        1st C
Gerald Jensen       Orlando    382-4391   Western    1st C
Scott J. Larsen     Calif      244-3566   Western    coach
Patty Little        Portland   244-2676   Western    1st C
Patricia Pace       Redding    821-2119   United     coach
Ted H. Pryor        New York   255-2954   TWA        coach
Conrad Silvers      D.C.       734-9132   TWA        coach
Robert R. Thompson  Holland    912-3356   United     coach
Cathy White         LA         433-6713   Western    coach


B:\PASSAGE.4                             Doc 1  Pg 1  Ln 1      Pos 10
```

The passenger list is now sorted alphabetically by last and first name.

Multiple-level Sort

You can divide people and things into groups and then sort within those groups. In this lesson, you divide a passenger list by airlines, then by class within each airline, then by last name, and finally, by first name—all in the same sort. You also learn how to sort a file from your disk.

While working through the lesson, you learn the following facts about WordPerfect's Sort feature:

• You can select the Sort feature from a clear screen, then retrieve a file from disk for sorting.

• The Delete key can be used to delete previous key definitions.

• You cannot delete the default definition for key 1.

The skills you learn in this lesson can be used for organizing and arranging lists of any kind.

26.1   Retrieve a document

Prepare to sort a passenger list from disk. Start with a clear screen.

Ctrl F9 , 2   Select the *Sort* option on the Merge/Sort menu to begin the Sort feature.

ENTER   **passage.1** as the filename for the Input file.

  Accept the option of sorting to the screen. PASSAGE.1 is retrieved to the screen and the Sort menu appears. If "Sort by Line" is not the Sort menu heading, press **7** for "Type" and **2** for "Line."

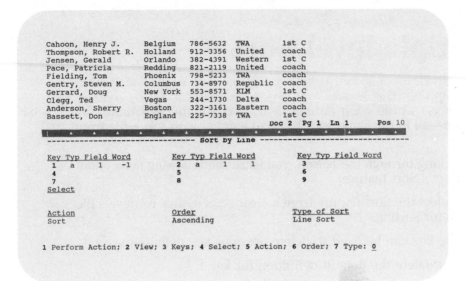

```
Cahoon, Henry J.      Belgium    786-5632   TWA       1st C
Thompson, Robert R.   Holland    912-3356   United    coach
Jensen, Gerald        Orlando    382-4391   Western   1st C
Pace, Patricia        Redding    821-2119   United    coach
Fielding, Tom         Phoenix    798-5233   TWA       coach
Gentry, Steven M.     Columbus   734-8970   Republic  coach
Gerrard, Doug         New York   553-8571   KLM       1st C
Clegg, Ted            Vegas      244-1730   Delta     coach
Anderson, Sherry      Boston     322-3161   Eastern   coach
Bassett, Don          England    225-7338   TWA       1st C
                                        Doc 2  Pg 1  Ln 1        Pos 10
```
--------------------------- Sort by Line --------------------------

```
Key Typ Field Word        Key Typ Field Word        Key Typ Field Word
  1   a    1    -1           2   a    1    1           3
  4                          5                         6
  7                          8                         9
Select


Action                    Order                     Type of Sort
Sort                      Ascending                 Line Sort

  1 Perform Action; 2 View; 3 Keys; 4 Select; 5 Action; 6 Order; 7 Type: 0
```

26.2

Define keys

Define four keys to sort PASSAGE.1 by airline, class, and last and first name.

3 Select the *Keys* option to define keys 1-4.

Del Press as many times as necessary to delete any previous key definitions. (You cannot delete the default setting for key1.)

As you define keys, use the Right and Left Arrow keys to move from entry to entry.

ENTER **a 4 1** for key1.

ENTER **a 5 1** for key2.

ENTER **a 1 1** for key3.

ENTER **a 1 2** for key4.

F7 Exit to the Sort menu.

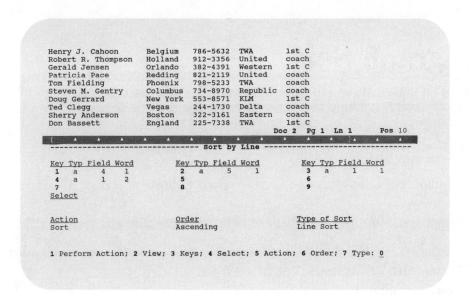

```
     Henry J. Cahoon       Belgium    786-5632   TWA        1st C
     Robert R. Thompson    Holland    912-3356   United     coach
     Gerald Jensen         Orlando    382-4391   Western    1st C
     Patricia Pace         Redding    821-2119   United     coach
     Tom Fielding          Phoenix    798-5233   TWA        coach
     Steven M. Gentry      Columbus   734-8970   Republic   coach
     Doug Gerrard          New York   553-8571   KLM        1st C
     Ted Clegg             Vegas      244-1730   Delta      coach
     Sherry Anderson       Boston     322-3161   Eastern    coach
     Don Bassett           England    225-7338   TWA        1st C
                                          Doc 2  Pg 1  Ln 1         Pos 10
  {        ▲        ▲       ▲      ▲      ▲         ▲         ]▲       ▲
  --------------------------------- Sort by Line ---------------------------------

  Key Typ Field Word        Key Typ Field Word        Key Typ Field Word
    1   a    4    1            2   a    5    1            3   a    1    1
    4   a    1    2            5                          6
    7                         8                          9
  Select

  Action                    Order                     Type of Sort
  Sort                      Ascending                 Line Sort

      1 Perform Action; 2 View; 3 Keys; 4 Select; 5 Action; 6 Order; 7 Type: 0
```

Begin sorting

You are now ready to sort the PASSAGE.1 file.

[1] Select the *Perform Action* option to begin sorting.

```
  Clegg, Ted            Vegas      244-1730   Delta      coach
  Anderson, Sherry      Boston     322-3161   Eastern    coach
  Hyde, Mary C.         Maine      225-1555   Frontier   coach
  Gerrard, Doug         New York   553-8571   KLM        1st C
  Collins, Fred         Calif      553-4981   Republic   coach
  Gentry, Steven M.     Columbus   734-8970   Republic   coach
  Bassett, Don          England    225-7338   TWA        1st C
  Cahoon, Henry J.      Belgium    786-5632   TWA        1st C
  Jacobs, Ronald        New York   373-2248   TWA        1st C
  Fielding, Tom         Phoenix    798-5233   TWA        coach
  Fields, Carl J.       Sweden     255-1076   TWA        coach
  Pryor, Ted H.         New York   255-2954   TWA        coach
  Silvers, Conrad       D.C.       734-9132   TWA        coach
  Pace, Patricia        Redding    821-2119   United     coach
  Thompson, Robert R.   Holland    912-3356   United     coach
  Curtis, Helen         LA         373-2604   Western    1st C
  Jensen, Gerald        Orlando    382-4391   Western    1st C
  Little, Patty         Portland   244-2676   Western    1st C
  Jacobs, Daniel        LA         322-7502   Western    coach
  Larsen, Scott J.      Calif      244-3566   Western    coach
  White, Cathy          LA         433-6713   Western    coach



                                      Doc 1  Pg 1  Ln 1       Pos 10
```

The passenger list is now sorted alphabetically by airline, then by class within each airline, and finally, by name within each class.

Lesson 27

Paragraph Sort

Paragraphs of information can also be sorted. In this lesson, you alphabetically sort a vacation list by the first word in the title of each holiday option.

While working through the lesson, you learn the following facts about WordPerfect's Sort feature:

- Each paragraph must end with two or more Hard Returns or a page break.

- The paragraph can be one line, several lines, or up to a page in length.

- Paragraph sorting requires a different type of sort.

The skills you learn in this lesson can be used for

- Sorting tables of authorities.
- Sorting class catalogs.
- Sorting merge files without the ^R's and ^E's.

27.1 Retrieve a document

Retrieve the vacation list onto the screen and prepare to sort it. Start with a clear screen.

 Select the Retrieve feature.

ENTER **trips.1** as the filename.

```
Stella Solaris   9-day Easter cruise to the Greek islands, Egypt,
Israel and Turkey.  Opportunity to see great spectacles of the
Aegean, while traveling in splendid luxury.

Stella Maris   7-day cruise around the coat of Italy.  Full of
delightful ports that cannot be reached by larger vessels.

Royal Princess   14-day cruise from Los Angeles to San Juan.
Filled with many happy memories:  music is sweeter, stars are
brighter, and the nights more romantic than ever before.

Island Princess   7-day cruise from Los Angeles to Acapulco.
You'll always remember this glittering pearl of the Mexican
Riviera.

Caravan   7-day Aegean cruise.  Includes all sightseeing shore
excursions operated at the classic quality level.

Continental   10-day tour of England, Belgium, Holland, Germany,
and France.  Experience this delightful corner of Europe, London
and the Kentish countryside.

Grand   15 days in Europe's scenic wonderland.  Imperial London,
Holland canals, Belgium, tiny Luxembourg and the allure of

B:\TRIPS.1                              Doc 1  Pg 1  Ln 1     Pos 10
```

`Ctrl` `F9` , `2` Select the *Sort* option on the Merge/Sort menu.

`↵` Accept the option of sorting the file on the screen.

`↵` Accept the option of sorting to the screen. The Sort menu appears on the bottom half of the screen.

27.2   Change types and define a key

Since sorting paragraphs is a different type of sort from sorting lines, you need to change types before defining keys.

`7` , `3` Select the *Paragraph* option on the Sorting Type menu.

`3` Select the *Keys* option to define key 1.

`Del` Press as many times as necessary to delete any previous key definitions.

After deleting all the key definitions, "a 1 1 1" appears for key1. This is the default setting for key1 and is the definition you need for the sort.

`F7` Exit to the Sort menu.

Begin sorting

You are now ready to sort the TRIPS.1 file.

[1] Select the *Perform Action* option to begin sorting.

```
Caravan    7-day Aegean cruise.  Includes all sightseeing shore
excursions operated at the classic quality level.

Continental   10-day tour of England, Belgium, Holland, Germany,
and France.  Experience this delightful corner of Europe, London
and the Kentish countryside.

Grand    15 days in Europe's scenic wonderland.  Imperial London,
Holland canals, Belgium, tiny Luxembourg and the allure of
Germany's Rhineland and Black Forest.

Island Princess    7-day cruise from Los Angeles to Acapulco.
You'll always remember this glittering pearl of the Mexican
Riviera.

Royal Princess    14-day cruise from Los Angeles to San Juan.
Filled with many happy memories:  music is sweeter, stars are
brighter, and the nights more romantic than ever before.

Stella Maris    7-day cruise around the coat of Italy.  Full of
delightful ports that cannot be reached by larger vessels.

Stella Solaris    9-day Easter cruise to the Greek islands, Egypt,
Israel and Turkey.  Opportunity to see great spectacles of the

B:\TRIPS.1                          Doc 1  Pg 1  Ln 1      Pos 10
```

If you have used the Paragraph Numbering feature in the document and want to sort records alphabetically by the first word, paragraph numbers are automatically renumbered.

Merge Sort

The Sort feature also recognizes the Merge codes of a secondary file for sorting. In this lesson, you numerically sort a secondary merge file by airfare. The records are retrieved from disk, sorted, and saved on disk.

While working through the lesson, you learn the following facts about WordPerfect's Sort feature:

- An Output file can be saved directly to disk.

- Sorting of merge files requires a different type of sort.

The skills you learn in this lesson can be used for organizing and arranging lists set up in a secondary merge file.

28.1   Retrieve a document

Prepare to sort a passenger list from disk. Start with a clear screen.

<kbd>Ctrl</kbd> <kbd>F9</kbd> , <kbd>2</kbd>   Select the *Sort* option on the Merge/Sort menu to begin the Sort feature.

ENTER   **passage.3** as the name for the Input file.

ENTER   **flight.1** as the name for the Output file. The Sort menu appears on the bottom half of the screen.

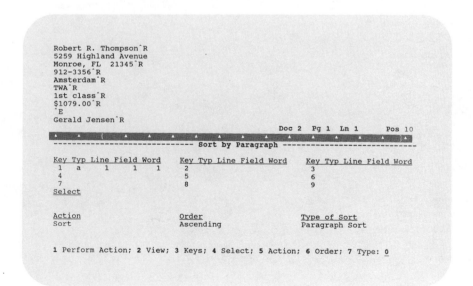

Change types and define a key

Since sorting merge files is a different type of sort from sorting lines or paragraphs, you need to change types before defining keys.

7 , 1   Select the *Merge* option on the Sorting Type menu.

3   Select the *Keys* option to define key 1.

Del   Press as many times as necessary to delete any previous key definitions.

ENTER   **n 7 1 1** for key1.

F7   Exit to the Sort menu.

28.3   **Begin sorting**

You are now ready to sort the PASSAGE.3 file.

1   Select the *Perform Action* option to begin sorting

28.4   **View the sorted file**

When the sort is finished, the sorted records are saved in the FLIGHT.1 file on disk. The Sort menu disappears and the screen is clear.

Shift F10   Select the Retrieve feature to view the sorted file.

ENTER   **flight.1** as the filename.

```
    Steven M. Jensen˘R
    190 W. 1100 S.
    Peoria, IL  50122˘R
    734-8970˘R
    Columbus, OH˘R
    Western˘R
    coach˘R
    $89.00˘R
    ˘E
    Tom Fielding˘R
    43 S. Orem Blvd.
    Salt Lake City, UT  84058˘R
    798-5233˘R
    Phoenix˘R
    Western˘R
    coach˘R
    $99.00˘R
    ˘E
    Daniel Jacobs˘R
    380 N. Gates
    Haleys, MO  55672˘R
    322-5702˘R
    New Orleans, LA˘R
    Delta˘R

    B:\FLIGHT.1                          Doc 1  Pg 1  Ln 1      Pos 10
```

Single-key Select and Sort

You can select specific file records which meet your criteria before you sort them. In this lesson, you select TWA passengers and then sort them alphabetically by last name.

While working through the lesson, you learn the following facts about WordPerfect's Sort feature:

- In the Select statement, spaces are not required between words and symbols.

- Keys must be defined before typing the Select statement.

- The equal sign (=) is a valid Select statement operator.

The skills you learn in this lesson can be used for selecting specific subgroups from larger lists, then organizing and arranging them.

29.1 Retrieve a document

Prepare to sort a passenger list from disk. Start with a clear screen.

Ctrl F9 , 2   Select the *Sort* option on the Merge/Sort menu to begin the Sort feature.

ENTER   **passage.1** as the filename for the Input file.

Accept the option of sorting to the screen. PASSAGE.1 is retrieved to the screen and the Sort menu appears. If "Sort by Line" is not the Sort menu heading, press **7** for "Type" and **2** for "Line."

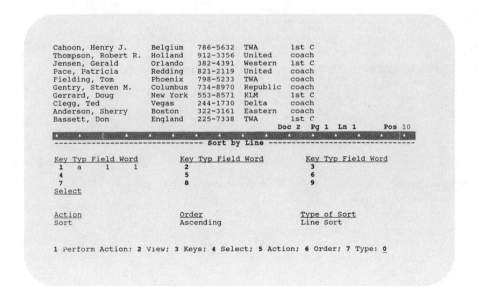

29.2 Define keys

Define two keys to sort certain passengers by last name. Keys must be defined before typing the Select statement.

3 Select the *Keys* option to define keys 1 and 2.

Del Press as many times as necessary to delete any previous key definitions. (You cannot delete the default setting for key1.)

As you define keys, use the Right and Left Arrow keys to move from entry to entry.

ENTER **a 1 1** for key1.

ENTER **a 4 1** for key2.

F7 Exit to the Sort menu.

29.3 Enter a Select statement

You must create a Select statement that asks for only the TWA passengers in the sort.

4 Select the *Select* option on the Sort menu to enter a Select statement.

Ctrl End Delete any previous Select statement.

ENTER **key2=twa** as the Select statement and return to the Sort menu.

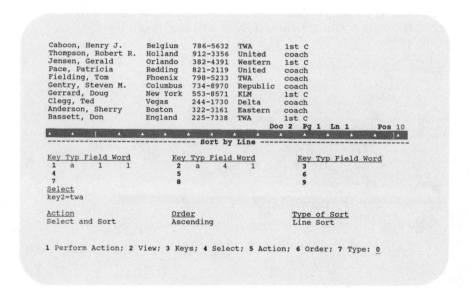

```
Cahoon, Henry J.       Belgium    786-5632   TWA        1st C
Thompson, Robert R.    Holland    912-3356   United     coach
Jensen, Gerald         Orlando    382-4391   Western    1st C
Pace, Patricia         Redding    821-2119   United     coach
Fielding, Tom          Phoenix    798-5233   TWA        coach
Gentry, Steven M.      Columbus   734-8970   Republic   coach
Gerrard, Doug          New York   553-8571   KLM        1st C
Clegg, Ted             Vegas      244-1730   Delta      coach
Anderson, Sherry       Boston     322-3161   Eastern    coach
Bassett, Don           England    225-7338   TWA        1st C
                                        Doc 2  Pg 1  Ln 1        Pos 10
------------------------------- Sort by Line -------------------------------

Key Typ Field Word       Key Typ Field Word       Key Typ Field Word
 1   a     1    1          2   a     4    1          3
 4                         5                         6
 7                         8                         9
Select
key2=twa

Action                   Order                    Type of Sort
Select and Sort          Ascending                Line Sort


1 Perform Action; 2 View; 3 Keys; 4 Select; 5 Action; 6 Order; 7 Type: 0
```

You are now ready to select and sort PASSAGE.1.

1 Select the *Perform Action* option to begin sorting.

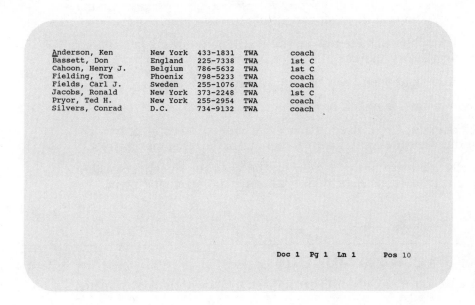

The list now includes only TWA passengers, arranged alphabetically by last name.

Lesson 30

Double-key Select and Sort

"Select statements" may have multiple parts which combine criteria for your selection. In this lesson, you select all TWA *and* United passengers, then sort them alphabetically by last name.

While working through the lesson, you learn the following facts about WordPerfect's Sort feature:

• Spaces are required between keys in a Select statement.

• Selection is done from left to right.

• The OR operator (+) is used in a Select statement to connect two key definitions when the conditions of either one *or* the other must be met.

The skills you learn in this lesson can be used for selecting specific subgroups from larger lists, then organizing and arranging them.

30.1   Retrieve a document

Prepare to sort a passenger list from disk. Start with a clear screen.

Ctrl F9 , 2   Select the *Sort* option on the Merge/Sort menu to begin the Sort feature.

ENTER   **passage.1** as the filename for the Input file.

↵   Accept the option of sorting to the screen. PASSAGE.1 is retrieved to the screen and the Sort menu appears. If "Sort by Line" is not the Sort menu heading, press **7** for "Type" and **2** for "Line."

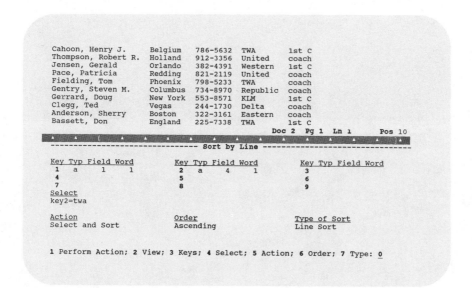

```
Cahoon, Henry J.     Belgium   786-5632   TWA        1st C
Thompson, Robert R.  Holland   912-3356   United     coach
Jensen, Gerald       Orlando   382-4391   Western    1st C
Pace, Patricia       Redding   821-2119   United     coach
Fielding, Tom        Phoenix   798-5233   TWA        coach
Gentry, Steven M.    Columbus  734-8970   Republic   coach
Gerrard, Doug        New York  553-8571   KLM        1st C
Clegg, Ted           Vegas     244-1730   Delta      coach
Anderson, Sherry     Boston    322-3161   Eastern    coach
Bassett, Don         England   225-7338   TWA        1st C
                                       Doc 2  Pg 1  Ln 1      Pos 10

----------------------------- Sort by Line -----------------------------

Key Typ Field Word        Key Typ Field Word        Key Typ Field Word
 1   a    1    1            2   a    4    1            3
 4                          5                          6
 7                          8                          9
Select
key2=twa

Action                    Order                     Type of Sort
Select and Sort           Ascending                 Line Sort

1 Perform Action; 2 View; 3 Keys; 4 Select; 5 Action; 6 Order; 7 Type: 0
```

30.2 Define keys

Define two keys to sort certain passengers by last name. Keys must be defined before typing the Select statement.

3 Select the *Keys* option to define keys 1 and 2.

Del Press as many times as necessary to delete any previous key definitions. (You cannot delete the default setting for key1.)

As you define keys, use the Right and Left Arrow keys to move from entry to entry.

ENTER **a 1 1** for key1.

ENTER **a 4 1** for key2.

F7 Exit to the Sort menu.

30.3 Enter a Select statement

You must create a Select statement that asks for the TWA *and* United passengers in the sort.

4 Select the *Select* option on the Sort menu to enter a Select statement.

Ctrl End Delete any previous Select statement.

ENTER **key2=twa + key2=united** as the Select statement and return to the Sort menu.

Begin sorting

You are now ready to select and sort PASSAGE.1.

1 Select the *Perform Action* option to begin sorting.

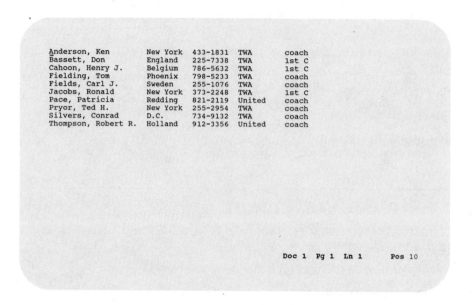

```
Anderson, Ken        New York   433-1831   TWA      coach
Bassett, Don         England    225-7338   TWA      1st C
Cahoon, Henry J.     Belgium    786-5632   TWA      1st C
Fielding, Tom        Phoenix    798-5233   TWA      coach
Fields, Carl J.      Sweden     255-1076   TWA      coach
Jacobs, Ronald       New York   373-2248   TWA      1st C
Pace, Patricia       Redding    821-2119   United   coach
Pryor, Ted H.        New York   255-2954   TWA      coach
Silvers, Conrad      D.C.       734-9132   TWA      coach
Thompson, Robert R.  Holland    912-3356   United   coach




                                                   Doc 1  Pg 1  Ln 1      Pos 10
```

The list now includes only TWA and United passengers, arranged alphabetically by last name.

Multiple-key Select and Sort

You can also select and sort a secondary merge file. In this lesson, you set up a Select statement that selects and sorts all TWA *and* United passengers who paid between $200 and $700 airfare.

While working through the lesson, you learn the following facts about WordPerfect's Sort feature:

- The part of a Select statement contained within parentheses takes precedence over the left to right selection order.

- The less than and greater than signs (< , >) are valid select operators.

- The AND operator (*) is used in a Select statement to connect two key definitions when the conditions of *both* must be met.

The skills you learn in this lesson can be used for selecting specific subgroups from larger lists, then organizing and arranging them.

 ## 31.1 Retrieve a document

Prepare to sort a passenger list from disk. Start with a clear screen.

Ctrl F9 , 2   Select the *Sort* option on the Merge/Sort menu to begin the Sort feature.

ENTER   **passage.3** as the filename for the Input file.

↵ Accept the option of sorting to the screen. PASSAGE.3 is retrieved to the screen and the Sort menu appears. If "Sort Secondary Merge File" is not the Sort menu heading, press **7** for "Type" and **1** for "Merge."

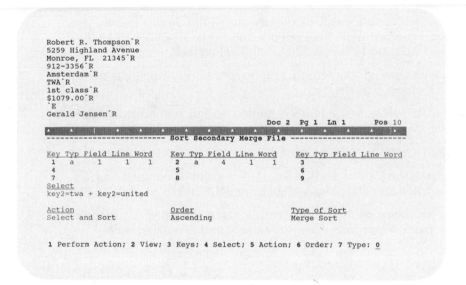

```
Robert R. Thompson^R
5259 Highland Avenue
Monroe, FL  21345^R
912-3356^R
Amsterdam^R
TWA^R
1st class^R
$1079.00^R
^E
Gerald Jensen^R
                                          Doc 2  Pg 1  Ln 1        Pos 10
▲    ▲    (    ▲    ▲    ▲    ▲    ▲    ▲    ▲    ▲    ▲    ▲    ▲    ▲
----------------------- Sort Secondary Merge File -----------------------

Key Typ Field Line Word    Key Typ Field Line Word    Key Typ Field Line Word
 1   a     1    1    1       2   a     4    1    1       3
 4                           5                           6
 7                           8                           9
Select
key2=twa + key2=united

Action                     Order                      Type of Sort
Select and Sort            Ascending                  Merge Sort


 1 Perform Action; 2 View; 3 Keys; 4 Select; 5 Action; 6 Order; 7 Type: 0
```

31.2 Define keys

Define three keys to sort by last name certain passengers who paid a certain airfare. Keys must be defined before typing the Select statement.

3 Select the *Keys* option to define keys 1-3.

Del Press as many times as necessary to delete any previous key definitions. (You cannot delete the default setting for key1.)

As you define keys, use the Right and Left Arrow keys to move from entry to entry.

ENTER **a 1 1 -1** for key1.

ENTER **a 5 1 1** for key2.

ENTER **n 7 1 1** for key3.

F7 Exit to the Sort menu.

31.3 Enter a Select statement

You must create a Select statement that asks for the TWA *and* United passengers who paid between $200 and $700 airfare.

4 Select the *Select* option on the Sort menu to enter a Select statement.

Delete any previous Select statement.

ENTER **(key2=twa + key2=united) * key3 > $200.00 * key3 < $700.00** as the Select statement and return to the Sort menu.

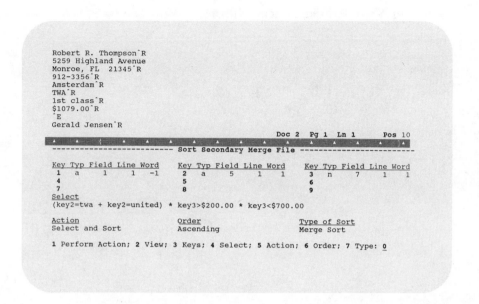

```
      Robert R. Thompson^R
      5259 Highland Avenue
      Monroe, FL  21345^R
      912-3356^R
      Amsterdam^R
      TWA^R
      1st class^R
      $1079.00^R
      ^E
      Gerald Jensen^R
                                          Doc 2   Pg 1   Ln 1       Pos 10

      ---------------------- Sort Secondary Merge File ----------------------

      Key Typ Field Line Word   Key Typ Field Line Word   Key Typ Field Line Word
       1  a    1    1   -1       2  a    5    1    1       3  n    7    1    1
       4                         5                         6
       7                         8                         9
      Select
      (key2=twa + key2=united)  *  key3>$200.00  *  key3<$700.00

      Action                    Order                     Type of Sort
      Select and Sort           Ascending                 Merge Sort

      1 Perform Action;  2 View;  3 Keys;  4 Select;  5 Action;  6 Order;  7 Type: 0
```

Begin sorting

You are now ready to select and sort PASSAGE.3.

1 Select the *Perform Action* option to begin sorting.

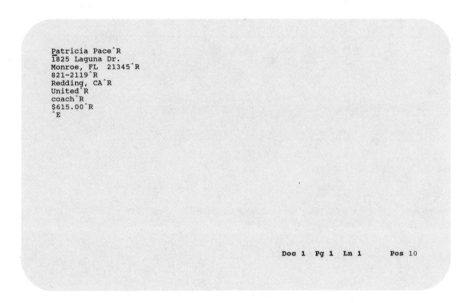

The list now includes only TWA and United passengers who paid between $200 and $700 airfare, arranged alphabetically by last name.

Combining Macros and Merges

You can save yourself some keystrokes during a merge by using macros to automate the process.

In this lesson, you merge a memo form (primary file) with the keyboard. The merge is started by a macro. After you have typed the memo, another macro sends the completed memo to the printer, then asks you for a filename by which you save the memo on disk.

While working through the lesson, you learn the following facts about macros and merges:

- You can start a merge with a macro.

- You can automatically start a macro at the end of each merged document.

The skills you learn in this lesson let you fully automate a merge process, from starting the merge to saving and printing the merged document.

32.1 The memo

The memo for this step is the primary file created in Lesson 10. We assume you have completed Lesson 10 and saved the primary file as MEMO on the Learning diskette/directory.

Remember that macros are saved as files on the default drive just like any other file. The macro, primary, secondary, and other needed files must be in the default drive or directory for the following example to work.

32.2 Define the MEMO macro

To begin, define a macro that starts the merge. The number of keystrokes needed to start the memo-merge is thereby reduced.

`Ctrl` `F10` Select the Macro Define feature to begin defining the "start" macro.

`ENTER` **memo** as the macro name.

`Ctrl` `F9` , `1` Select the *Merge* option on the Merge menu to start the merge.

ENTER **memo** as the primary file.

⏎ There is no secondary file. Merging begins.

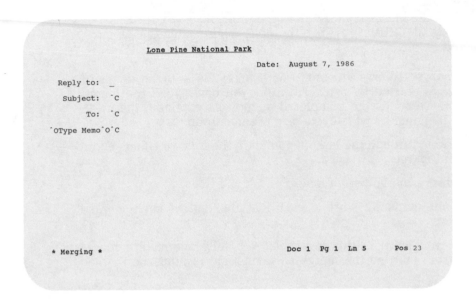

Shift F9 Select the Merge E feature to end the merge.

32.3 Define the END macro

Now, define a macro that automatically sends the finished memo to the printer and then requests a filename for saving the memo.

Ctrl F10 Select the Macro Define feature to define the "print and save" macro.

ENTER **end** as the macro name.

Shift F7 , 1 Select the *Full Text* option on the Print menu to print a document.

F7 , Y Begin saving the memo.

Ctrl F10 Select the Macro Define feature to end the macro definition.

F1 Cancel the "Document to be Saved:" message.

F7 , N , ⏎ Clear the screen.

The memo could also be appended (using the Append feature) to a MEMO file for future reference instead of having each memo in a separate file.

32.4　Prepare the primary file

There are specific merge commands that tell a primary file to start a macro after the merge is finished. In this case, insert a code that tells the primary file MEMO to start the END macro after the memo is completed.

[Shift] [F10]　Select the Retrieve feature.

ENTER　**memo** as the filename. The memo appears on the screen.

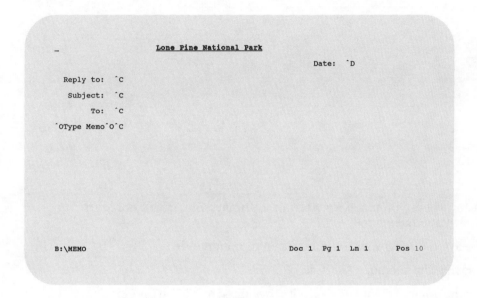

```
               _            Lone Pine National Park

                                              Date:  ^D

        Reply to:  ^C
         Subject:  ^C
             To:  ^C
    ^OType Memo^O^C
```

B:\MEMO   Doc 1 Pg 1 Ln 1   Pos 10

[Alt] [F9] , [G]　Select the Merge Codes feature and insert ^G into the memo.

TYPE　**end** (this is the name of the macro just created).

Alt F9 , G Select the Merge Codes feature and insert ^G into the memo. You should see ^Gend^G at the top of the memo.

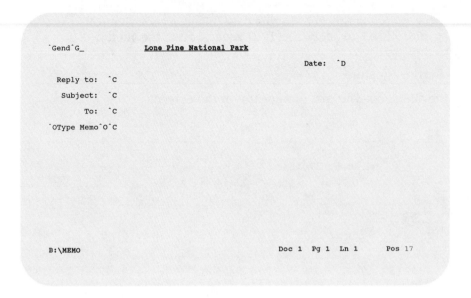

No matter where you place a macro in a primary file, it will not start until the merge has ended.

Now, resave the memo with the new merge commands.

F7 , Y Begin saving the memo.

↵ , Y Replace the original memo on disk with the edited memo on the screen.

↵ Clear the screen.

32.5 Start the macro and merge

When you are ready to run the macro and merge,

Alt F10 Select the Macro feature, and you are asked for the macro name.

ENTER **memo** as the macro name. The macro begins by starting your memo merge.

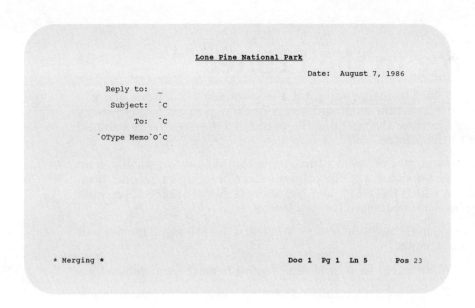

```
                      Lone Pine National Park

                                          Date:  August 7, 1986

        Reply to:  _

         Subject:  ^C

             To:  ^C

     ^OType Memo^O^C




     * Merging *                    Doc 1  Pg 1  Ln 5      Pos 23
```

After typing an entry, press the Merge R key to continue the merge. As soon as you complete the memo, it is sent to the printer, after which you are asked to type a filename for the memo. Enter a filename, then clear the screen.

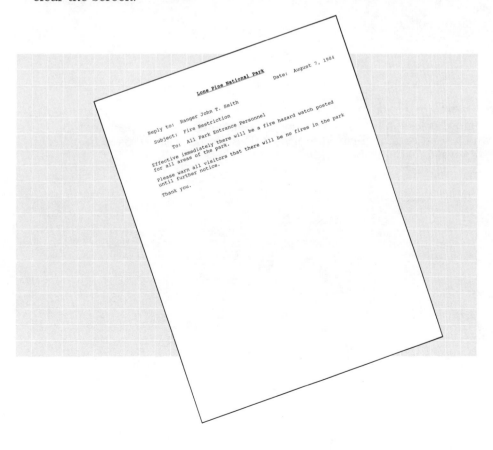

```
                      Lone Pine National Park      Date:  August 7, 1984

        Reply to:  Ranger John T. Smith

         Subject:  Fire Restriction

             To:  All Park Entrance Personnel

     Effective immediately there will be a fire hazard watch posted
     for all areas of the park.

     Please warn all visitors that there will be no fires in the park
     until further notice.

     Thank you.
```

Lesson 33

Merge to the Printer

When you need to merge and print a large number of letters, and you either don't have time to sit and watch, or there is not enough memory and disk space for the resulting file of merged documents, you should merge to the printer.

In this lesson, you create a primary file that will automatically send each merged document to the printer before creating a new one. Both the primary file LETTER.PF and the address file ADDRESS.SF created in Lesson 9 are necessary for this lesson.

Hand-fed forms cannot be used while merging to the printer.

While working through the lesson, you learn the following facts about merge commands:

- ^N tells WordPerfect to get the next record from the secondary file.
- ^T tells WordPerfect to send all text merged to that point to the printer.
- ^P*filename*^P tells WordPerfect to start the merge over using the primary file named between ^P's.

The skills you learn in this lesson can be used to print

- Mass mailing letters.
- Labels.
- Organization notices.

33.1 Change the primary file

You begin this lesson by inserting merge commands into the primary file which send each letter to the printer. The file LETTER.PF used in this step was created in Lesson 9.

Shift F10 Select the Retrieve feature.

ENTER letter.pf as the filename.

```
ˆF1ˆ
ˆF2ˆ
ˆF3ˆ

Dear ˆF5ˆ:

     Thank you, ˆF5ˆ, for an outstanding effort in fighting the
largest fire in Lone Pine National Park's history.  The volunteer
fire fighters in your community are an inspiring model for all
fire fighters in our state and nation.

With appreciation,


Ranger John T. Smith




B:\LETTER.PF                              Doc 1  Pg 1  Ln 1      Pos 10
```

Home , Home , ↓ Move to the end of the document.

↵ Return the cursor to the next line.

Alt F9 , T Select the Merge Codes feature and insert ^T into the primary file.

^T sends all text merged to that point to the printer.

Alt F9 , N Select the Merge Codes feature and insert ^N into the primary file.

^N tells the merge to go to the next record in the secondary file.

Alt F9 , P Select the Merge Codes feature and insert ^P into the primary file.

^P tells the merge to start over again.

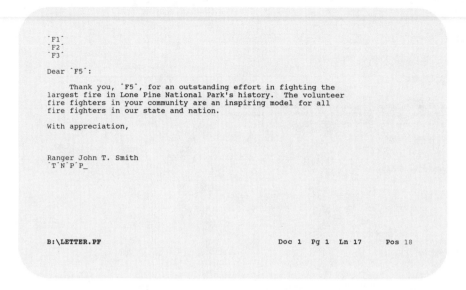

Alt F9 , P Select the Merge Codes feature and insert another ^P to complete the pair.

The pair of ^P's tells the merge which primary file to use next. Because a primary file is not named between the two ^P's, WordPerfect uses the same primary file again.

The ^N^P^P combination tells WordPerfect not to insert an extra page break since the printer will automatically advance to the next page when it finishes each letter.

F7 , Y Begin saving the file.

ENTER **merge1** as the filename.

↵ Clear the screen.

Start the merge

The secondary file ADDRESS.SF used in this merge was created in Lesson 9.

Ctrl F9 , 1   Select the *Merge* option on the Merge/Sort menu.

ENTER   **merge1** as the primary file.

ENTER   **address.sf** as the secondary file.

The screen is cleared and merging to the printer begins.

Lesson 34

 Reports and Lists

Lists and reports can be generated by customizing the merge. In this lesson, you create a name and phone list using the secondary file ADDRESS.SF that was created in Lesson 9.

While working through the lesson, you learn the following facts about the Merge feature:

- A secondary file can be used for more than just a simple merge.

- You can adjust the format of a document after it has been merged.

The skills you learn in this lesson can be used to generate lists and reports.

34.1 | The primary file

Begin by typing and saving the following primary file as PHONE.LST.

TYPE **^F1^[TAB]^F4^[HRt]**
      ^N^P^P

Press the Enter key when you see [HRt] and press the Tab key when you see [TAB].

The ^N^P^P combination tells WordPerfect not to insert an extra page break since the printer will automatically advance to the next page when it finishes each letter.

F7 , Y   Begin saving the primary file.

ENTER **phone.lst** as the filename.

⏎   Clear the screen.

34.2 | Start the merge

You are ready to create a phone list with the Merge feature.

Ctrl F9 , 1   Select the *Merge* option on the Merge/Sort menu to start the merge.

ENTER **phone.lst** as the primary file.

ENTER **address.sf** as the secondary file. "Merge" appears on the status line until the merge is completed.

<table>
<tr><td>**34.3**</td><td>

Adjust the format

</td></tr>
</table>

After creating a list, you can adjust the format and add titles to finish editing the document. Set a tab for the phone numbers in the merged document.

MOVE To the beginning of the document.

Shift F8 , 1   Select the *Tabs* option on the Line Format menu, and the Tabs menu is displayed.

Ctrl End   Erase all the tab stops (beginning at position 10) using the Delete EOL feature.

ENTER **40** to insert a tab stop.

[F7] Exit the Tabs menu. The phone numbers move to position 40.

```
Mr. Alan Wilson          801 666-4545
Mr. Jeff Richards        801 666-6767
Mr. John Elliot




                                          Doc 1  Pg 1  Ln 1     Pos 10
```

Merge–Document Assembly 1

In this lesson, several paragraphs (each in a separate file) are used to "assemble" a contract. You select the paragraphs as you go.

While working through the lesson, you learn the following facts about Merge codes:

- ^U updates the screen so you can see the added text as the merge progresses.

- ^P^C^P lets you enter a file to be retrieved at that point.

- Placing ^P^C^P between two ^O's lets you display a reminder of what your options are at that point in the merge.

The skills you learn in this lesson can be used to create customized contracts.

35.1 | Create seven files

The steps below help you create seven files. The name of each file is a single character such as "3" or "T". After saving a file with the Exit key, clear the screen before starting the next file.

Press the Enter key when you see [HRt], and press the Tab key when you see [TAB].

TYPE **Two bedrooms with one and one-half bathrooms[HRt]**
[TAB]B.[TAB]^U^OEnter k for kitchen or t for
kitchenette:^P^C^P^O

The document should look like this:

```
Two bedrooms with one and one-half bathrooms
     B.   ˆUˆOEnter k for kitchen or t for kitchenette:ˆPˆCˆPˆO_




                                        Doc 1  Pg 1  Ln 2      Pos 73
```

F7, **Y**   Begin saving the file.

ENTER **2** as the filename.

⏎   Clear the screen.

TYPE   **Three bedrooms with one and three-quarters bathrooms[HRt]**
[TAB]B.[TAB]^U^OEnter k for kitchen or t for
kitchenette:^P^C^P^O

F7, **Y**   Begin saving the file.

ENTER **3** as the filename.

⏎   Clear the screen.

TYPE   **Four bedrooms with two full bathrooms[HRt]**
[TAB]B.[TAB]^U^OEnter k for kitchen or t for
kitchenette:^P^C^P^O

F7, **Y**   Begin saving the file.

ENTER **4** as the filename.

⏎   Clear the screen.

TYPE   **Kitchen including appliances[HRt]**
[TAB]C.[TAB]^U^OEnter s for pool or h for hot tub:^P^C^P^O

F7, **Y**   Begin saving the file.

ENTER **k** as the filename.

⏎   Clear the screen.

TYPE   **Kitchenette with no appliances[HRt]**
[TAB]C.[TAB]^U^OEnter s for pool or h for hot tub:^P^C^P^O

F7, **Y**   Begin saving the file.

ENTER **t** as the filename.

⏎   Clear the screen.

TYPE   **Swimming Pool**

F7, **Y**   Begin saving the file.

ENTER **s** as the filename.

⏎   Clear the screen.

TYPE   **Hot Tub**

F7, **Y**   Begin saving the file.

ENTER **h** as the filename.

⏎   Clear the screen.

35.2 The primary file

Now, type and save the following primary file as MERGE2.

TYPE   **I.[TAB]Property Description[HRt]**
[TAB]A.[TAB]^U^OEnter the number of bedrooms (2-4):
^P^C^P^O

A page break followed by ^Pmerge2^P would loop the merge over and over again until the Merge E key was pressed.

`F7` , `Y`   Begin saving the file.

ENTER   **merge2** as the filename.

↵   Clear the screen.

35.3 Start the merge

You are now ready to assemble the document.

`Ctrl` `F9` , `1`   Select the *Merge* option on the Merge/Sort menu.

ENTER   **merge2** as the primary file.

↵   Do not enter a secondary file, and begin merging.

```
    I.   Property Description
         A.   ^OEnter the number of bedrooms (2-4):^P^C^P^O













    Enter the number of bedrooms (2-4):_
```

You can now choose from the options displayed at the bottom left of the screen and press the Merge R key to continue.

Lesson 36

Merge–Document Assembly 2

The next three lessons introduce recursive (looping) properties of macros and merging. Complete these lessons only after you feel comfortable with most of the features in the previous macro and merge lessons.

In this lesson, you learn another method of assembling documents.

While working through the lesson, you learn the following facts about macros and merging:

- Hard Return codes [HRt] and Tab codes [TAB] can be placed in secondary records to format a primary file when merged.

- You can selectively merge fields containing sentences or paragraphs.

The skills you learn in this lesson can be used to produce a tailored document.

36.1   The secondary file

The file you create (shown below) contains only one record with nine fields. Some fields are only two lines long; some are as long as six lines.

TYPE **Fishing at Lone Pine National Park during[HRt]**
[TAB]^R
March 1 - August 31[HRt]
[HRt]
Fish in season:[HRt]
^F8^^R
September 1 - February 28[HRt]
[HRt]
Fish in season:[HRt]
^F9^^R
Lone Pine Reservoir is stocked with[HRt]
^F7^^R
Hard Rock River is stocked with[HRt]
^F6^^R
[TAB]Rainbow trout[HRt]
[TAB]German Brown trout[HRt]
[TAB]Bass[HRt]
[HRt]
^R

Press the Enter key when you see [HRt], and press the Tab key when you see [TAB].

[TAB]Perch[HRt]
[TAB]Lake trout[HRt]
[TAB]Catfish[HRt]
[TAB]Sunfish[HRt]
[TAB]Freshwater shark[HRt]
[HRt]
^R
[TAB]Rainbow trout[HRt]
[TAB]German Brown trout[HRt]
[TAB]Perch[HRt]
[TAB]Lake trout[HRt]
[TAB]Catfish[HRt]
[HRt]
^R
[TAB]Bass[HRt]
[TAB]Salmon[HRt]
[TAB]Sunfish[HRt]
[TAB]Freshwater shark[HRt]
[HRt]
^R
^E

The document should look like this:

```
 ˆR
       Perch
       Lake trout
       Catfish
       Sunfish
       Freshwater shark

 ˆR
       Rainbow trout
       German Brown trout
       Perch
       Lake trout
       Catfish

 ˆR
       Bass
       Salmon
       Sunfish
       Freshwater shark

 ˆR
 ˆE

 _


                              Doc 1   Pg 1   Ln 41      Pos 10
```

F7, Y Begin saving the document.

ENTER **fishing.sf** as the filename.

↵ Clear the screen.

36.2 The primary file

Now, create the following primary file. To type the ^F Merge code, hold down the Ctrl key and type **f**.

TYPE **^U^F^C^ ^P^P**

Use Shift ^ to add the extra control symbol.

F7, Y Begin saving the document.

ENTER **doc.pf** as the filename.

↵ Clear the screen.

36.3 Start the merge

You are now ready to merge the contents of the primary and secondary files.

Ctrl F9, 1 Select the *Merge* option on the Merge/Sort menu to start the merge.

ENTER **doc.pf** as the primary file.

ENTER **fishing.sf** as the secondary file.

```
^F^C^ ^P^P




















Field Number? _
```

The ^F^C lets you choose a field. Enter the number of the field. Press the Merge E key when you want to stop.

36.4 Use the merge

Create the following documents by starting the merge and entering the field numbers below.

Document 1	**Document 2**
Enter **1**	Enter **1**
Enter **2**	Enter **2**
Enter **4**	Enter **1**
Press the Merge E key	Enter **3**
	Enter **4**
	Enter **5**
	Press the Merge E Key

A completed Document 1 looks like this:

```
Fishing at Lone Pine National Park during
    March 1 - August 31

Fish in season:
    Rainbow trout
    German Brown trout
    Perch
    Lake trout
    Catfish

Lone Pine Reservoir is stocked with
    Perch
    Lake trout
    Catfish
    Sunfish
    Freshwater shark

_



                                      Doc 1  Pg 1  Ln 18     Pos 10
```

Try your own combination!

Lesson 37

 # Merge—Boilerplates

In this lesson, you build a flexible contract using previously created files. You should have completed Lesson 34 before starting this lesson.

While working through the lesson, you learn the following facts about the Merge feature:

- ^V lets you transfer Merge codes into the document being created.

- You can create a primary file which, when merged with itself, creates a secondary file.

The skills you learn in this lesson can be used to create and add to secondary files at the same time you create merge documents.

37.1 Create a file

To begin this lesson, create and save the following short file so that it is on disk when you create the "form" macro in section 35.4.

TYPE **customer file**

`F7` , `Y` Begin saving the text.

ENTER **customer** as the filename.

`↵` Clear the screen.

37.2 The first primary file

Now, duplicate the file you see on the screen below. This primary file is the basic *contract* used in the merge.

```
                    Lone Pine Recreational Property

Owner/Buyer ^F1^

^F1^ hereby deposits with Lone Pine Recreational Property as
EARNEST MONEY, the amount of $^F4^ which shall be deposited in
accordance with applicable State Law.

Type of Cabin: ^F2^

                        OFFER TO PURCHASE

I.   Property Description

     A.   ^U^OEnter the number of bedrooms (2-4): ^P^C^P^O

II.  Purchase Price and Financing

     The Total Price is $^F3^


          _____
                    ^F1^_


                              Doc 1  Pg 1  Ln 23     Pos 44
```

F7 , Y	Begin saving the document.
ENTER	**merge4** as the filename.
↵	Clear the screen.

37.3   The second primary file

Duplicate the file you see on the screen below. This primary file is used to create a secondary file with one record to be merged with the *contract*.

To insert ^R and ^E into this document without having the cursor return to the following line, hold down the Control key, then type **r** or **e**.

```
`OType Applicant's Full Name`O`C`V`R`V
`OType the Style of Cabin`O`C`V`R`V
`OType the Total Purchase Price`O`C`V`R`V
`OType the Amount of Earnest Money Deposited`O`C`V`R`V
`V`E`V
`Gform`G_
```

Doc 1   Pg 1   Ln 6   Pos 18

F7 , Y	Begin saving the document.
ENTER	**merge3** as the filename.
↵	Clear the screen.

37.4   Create a macro

This macro is started after the secondary record is created. The secondary file with the single record is saved, then merged with the "contract" primary file.

TYPE	**This is a test**
Ctrl F10	Select the Macro Define feature to begin defining a macro.
ENTER	**form**
Alt F4	Turn on Block.
Home , Home , ↑	Move to the beginning of the document
F10	Select the Save feature. You are asked for the block name.
ENTER	**customer** as the filename. You are asked to confirm the replacement of the original version of the CUSTOMER file you created in section 35.1.
Y	Confirm the replacement.
Alt F4	Turn off Block.

F7 , N , ↵	Clear the screen.
Ctrl F9 , 1	Select the *Merge* option on the Merge/Sort menu to start the merge.
ENTER	**merge4** as the primary file.
ENTER	**customer** as the secondary file.
	Don't enter any requested information.
Shift F9	End the merge with the Merge E feature.
F7 , N , ↵	Clear the screen.

37.5   Start the merge

You can now run the merge.

Ctrl F9 , 1	Select the *Merge* option on the Merge/Sort menu to start the merge.
ENTER	**merge3** as the primary file.
↵	Do not enter a secondary file (one has not been created yet).

```
^V^R^V
^OType the Style of Cabin^O^C^V^R^V
^OType the Total Purchase Price^O^C^V^R^V
^OType the Amount of Earnest Money Deposited^O^C^V^R^V
^V^E^V
^Gform^G




Type Applicant's Full Name                    Doc 1  Pg 1  Ln 1      Pos 10
```

Enter the information requested by the prompts, then press the Merge R key.

You could have created a macro that appended all contracts to a central file, or printed them, or both.

Lesson 38

 # Merge—Menus

In this lesson, you create a menu that lets you choose from a number of existing macros, each of which performs a different function. This lesson uses existing macros on the Learning diskette (1X.MAC, 2X.MAC ... 5X.MAC).

While working through the lesson, you learn the following facts about the Merge feature:

- You can insert more than one line of information between ^O codes to create multiple line prompts.

- You can insert ^C between ^G codes and the merge will stop to let you enter the name of the macro to be executed at the end of the merge.

The skills you learn in this lesson can be used to create menus from which you can select alternatives for the current merge.

38.1 The primary file

Duplicate the file you see on the screen below.

```
˙OMENU

1 - Format for an eighty column line printer

2 - Send the document to two printers

3 - Select an Epson eighty column printer

4 - Print five copies of the document

5 - Exit

Enter Selection (1-5):  ˙G˙Cx˙G˙O_



                                          Doc 1  Pg 1  Ln 13     Pos 43
```

[F7] , [Y] Begin saving the document.

ENTER **menu.pf** as the filename.

[↵] Clear the screen.

38.2 Start the merge

Since the macro files used with this merge already exist on the Learning diskette, you can start the merge.

[Ctrl] [F9] , [1] Select the *Merge* option on the Merge/Sort menu to start the merge.

ENTER **menu.pf** as the primary file.

[↵] There is no secondary file.

The following menu appears on the screen:

```
MENU

1 - Format for an eighty column line printer

2 - Send the document to two printers

3 - Select an Epson eighty column printer

4 - Print five copies of the document

5 - Exit

Enter Selection (1-5): _
```

ENTER The numbers requested by the prompts. Each time you enter a number, it invokes the corresponding "X.MAC" file on disk.

Lesson 39

Simple Math

The Math feature lets you perform several kinds of math calculations in a document. You can use the Math feature in all or part of the document. In this lesson, you create a simple math document that uses operators in a Numeric column for totaling numbers.

While working through the lesson, you learn the following facts about WordPerfect's Math feature.

- Tab stops delimit math columns.
- The space between the left margin and the first tab stop is not considered a math column and can be used for text.
- Text columns are used for inserting textual information like labels or titles.
- Numeric columns let you generate subtotals (+), totals (=), and grand totals (*).
- To insert extra subtotals and totals into a column, type "t" in front of a subtotal and "T" in front of a total.
- Total columns are a special type of numeric column. They are used to display totals from the column to the left.
- Numbers are aligned by the decimal point in numeric and total columns.
- You can turn Math on and off at any position in a document.
- Though operators (+, –, =, etc.) appear on the screen in a math document, they are not printed.

The skills you learn in this lesson can be used to create any document that includes a table or chart in which addition or subtraction is needed to generate totals.

39.1 Set a tab stop

Before turning on Math, you set a tab stop for a single Numeric column.

F7 , N , ↵   Clear the screen.

Shift F8 , 1   Select the *Tabs* option on the Line Format menu to display the Tabs menu.

Ctrl End   Erase all the tab stops (beginning at position 10) using the Delete EOL feature.

ENTER   **20** to set a tab stop.

F7   Exit the Tabs menu.

Turn on Math

Begin the math document by turning on the Math feature. Because each column is already set for Numeric, you do not need to create a definition.

`Alt` `F7` , `1` Select the *Math On* option on the Math menu. The "Math" message appears at the bottom of the screen.

```
Math                              Doc 1  Pg 1  Ln 1     Pos 10
```

39.3 Add "200" and "300"

Now, calculate a subtotal with the "+" operator.

`Tab` Insert a Tab which moves you to the Numeric column and begins aligning. The "Align Char =" message appears at the bottom of the screen.

TYPE **200.00**

`↵` End the current line and return the cursor to the next line.

`Tab` Insert a Tab which moves the cursor to the Numeric column and begins aligning.

TYPE **300.00**

`↵` End the current line and return the cursor to the next line.

`Tab` Insert a Tab which moves the cursor to the Numeric column and begins aligning.

TYPE **+** to create a subtotal.

⏎ Press 2 times to end the current line and add a blank line.

Alt F7 , 2 Select the *Calculate* option on the Math menu to calculate the subtotal. A result of "500.00" appears next to the "+" operator.

```
      200.00
      300.00
      500.00+



    _








Math                                    Doc 1  Pg 1  Ln 5      Pos 10
```

39.4 Add two negative numbers

Create another subtotal by adding two negative numbers. Notice that you can use a minus sign or parentheses to indicate a negative number.

Tab Insert a Tab which moves the cursor to the Numeric column and begins aligning.

TYPE **-150.00**

⏎ , Tab End the current line and insert a Tab. The cursor moves to the next line of the Numeric column.

TYPE **(25.00)**

⏎ , Tab End the current line and insert a Tab. The cursor moves to the next line of the Numeric column.

TYPE **+** to create a subtotal.

⏎ Press 2 times to end the current line and add a blank line.

Alt F7 , 2 Select the *Calculate* option on the Math menu to calculate the subtotal. A result of "(175.00)" appears next to the "+" operator. You can also define negative results to appear with a minus sign instead of parentheses.

39.5   Calculate a total

Continue by using the "=" operator to calculate a total from the two subtotals in the Numeric column.

Tab   Insert a Tab which moves the cursor to the Numeric column.

TYPE   **=** to create a total.

↵   End the current line and return the cursor to the next line.

Alt F7 , 2   Select the *Calculate* option on the Math menu to calculate the total.

A result of "325.00" appears next to the "=" operator.

39.6   Calculate a grand total

Insert an extra total, then use the "*" operator to calculate a grand total for the math document.

Tab   Insert a Tab which moves the cursor to the Numeric column and begins aligning.

TYPE   **T2,000.00** to insert an extra total.

↵   Press 2 times to end the current line and add a blank line.

Tab   Insert a Tab which moves the cursor to the Numeric column and begins aligning.

TYPE   ***** to create a grand total.

↵   Press 2 times to end the current line and add a blank line.

<kbd>Alt</kbd> <kbd>F7</kbd> , <kbd>2</kbd>   Select the *Calculate* option on the Math menu to calculate the grand total. WordPerfect calculates the two totals and a result of "2,325.00" appears next to the "*" operator.

```
        500.00+

       -150.00
        (25.00)
       (175.00)+

        325.00=
    T2,000.00

      2,325.00*




    -



Math                                    Doc 1  Pg 1  Ln 14      Pos 10
```

39.7 Print the document

To complete the lesson, turn off Math, then print the math document.

<kbd>Alt</kbd> <kbd>F7</kbd> , <kbd>1</kbd>   Select the *Math Off* option on the Math menu. The "Math" message disappears from the screen.

<kbd>Alt</kbd> <kbd>F3</kbd>   Display the Reveal Codes screen. Find the Math Off code [Math Off]. The cursor is to the right of it. At this point, you are outside of the math document.

<kbd>←</kbd>   Move inside the math document. The "Math" message appears again because the cursor is back inside the math document. Notice that any math operators blink in the Reveal Codes screen.

<kbd>→</kbd>   Move back outside the math document.

<kbd>Space Bar</kbd>   Exit the Reveal Codes screen and return to the normal screen.

Shift F7 , 1 TYPE Select the *Full Text* option on the Print menu to print the document. The operators (+,=,T,*) are not printed because WordPerfect identifies them as codes that are not sent to the printer.

200.00
300.00
500.00

-150.00
(25.00)
(175.00)

325.00
2,000.00

2,325.00

Lesson 40

Advanced Math

The Math feature also allows you to do more than just total numbers. You can define up to four Calculation columns in your math document and create one formula per column.

In this lesson, you update a financial statement for the Lone Pine Crafts store.

While working through the lesson, you learn the following facts about WordPerfect's Math feature:

- You can edit a math document.

- You can define up to four calculation columns in a math document.

- Each calculation column can include one formula using addition (+), subtraction (-), multiplication (*), and division (/).

- "!" is an operator inserted by WordPerfect, indicating that the formula for the column will be calculated for the current line. Delete "!" if you do not want a calculation for that line.

- WordPerfect calculates formulas across columns.

The skills you learn in this lesson can be used to create any documents that require mathematic calculations—even small spreadsheets.

40.1 Retrieve a document

Begin by retrieving the financial statement for the Lone Pine Crafts store.

 Select the Retrieve feature.

ENTER **crafts.lrn** as the filename.

```
                        Lone Pine Crafts

                        Quarter Revenues

Item              Revenues    Year to Date    Sales Tax    Order

Indian Rugs
   Small           500.00                       25.00!      Yes
   Medium          475.00                       23.75!      Yes
   Large           350.00                       17.50!      No
      Total      1,325.00+

Local Crafts
   Paintings     2,250.00                      112.50!      Yes
   Quilts          700.00                       35.00!      No
      Total      2,950.00+

Imports
   Toys          1,500.00                       75.00!      Yes
   Hats            850.00                       42.50!      No
      Total      2,350.00+                     331.25+

Quarter Total                   6,625.00=
   1st Quarter                 T3,275.00


B:\CRAFTS.LRN                               Doc 1  Pg 1  Ln 1      Pos 10
```

40.2

Change the amount of revenue from Indian Rugs, then calculate the financial statement.

MOVE To Line 10 Position 32.

Del Delete the characters "350".

TYPE **1,000** for the new amount of revenue from Indian Rugs.

<kbd>Alt</kbd> <kbd>F7</kbd> , <kbd>2</kbd> Select the *Calculate* option on the Math menu to calculate the financial statement. Several totals change, including the sales tax figures.

```
                        Lone Pine Crafts

                        Quarter Revenues

   Item               Revenues     Year to Date    Sales Tax    Order

   Indian Rugs
      Small             500.00                        25.00!     Yes
      Medium            475.00                        23.75!     Yes
      Large           1,000.00                        50.00!     No
         Total        1,975.00+

   Local Crafts
      Paintings       2,250.00                       112.50!     Yes
      Quilts            700.00                        35.00!     No
         Total        2,950.00+

   Imports
      Toys            1,500.00                        75.00!     Yes
      Hats              850.00                        42.50!     No
         Total        2,350.00+                      363.75+

   Quarter Total                    7,275.00=
      1st Quarter                  T3,275.00

   Math                                          Doc 1  Pg 1  Ln 10     Pos 35
```

40.3

Add Wood Carvings to the financial statement, enter the new figures, then calculate.

MOVE To Line 16 Position 10.

<kbd>↵</kbd> Add a blank line.

<kbd>↑</kbd> Move to the new blank line.

<kbd>Space Bar</kbd> Press 3 times to indent.

TYPE **Wood Carvings**

<kbd>Tab</kbd> Insert a Tab which moves the cursor to the Revenues column.

TYPE **625.00**

<kbd>Tab</kbd> Press 3 times to insert three Tabs which move the cursor to the Order column. The "!" operator automatically appears in the Calculation column.

<kbd>Alt</kbd> <kbd>F7</kbd> , <kbd>2</kbd> Select the *Calculate* option on the Math menu to calculate the financial statement.

40.4 Create a new definition

The sales tax changes from 5 to 6 percent. You need to update the sales tax figures on the financial statement. You can do this by simply creating a new definition that includes an updated sales tax formula.

Shift F2	Select the ◀Search feature.
Alt F7 , 1	Insert a [Math Def] code into the search.
F2	Begin the search.
Alt F7 , 2	Select the *Math Define* option on the Math menu to display the Math Definition menu.
→	Press 2 times to move to the Type number under column C.
TYPE	**0** for a Calculation column.
ENTER	**a*.06** to replace the old sales tax formula.

While you are in the definition, you also want to change the number of digits displayed in the Revenues column for the subtotals.

←	Press 3 times to move to column A.
↓	Press 2 times to move to the # of Digits category.
TYPE	**0** for the number of digits.
F7 , ↵	Exit the Math Definition menu and return to the math document.
←	Move next to the original Math definition.
Backspace , Y	Delete the original Math definition.
↓	Press 2 times to move into the financial statement.

| Alt | F7 | , | 2 | Select the *Calculate* option on the Math menu to calculate the financial statement.

```
                        Lone Pine Crafts

                        Quarter Revenues

Item                Revenues    Year to Date    Sales Tax    Order
Indian Rugs
    Small             500.00                       30.00!      Yes
    Medium            475.00                       28.50!      Yes
    Large           1,000.00                       60.00!      No
        Total       1,975+

Local Crafts
    Paintings       2,250.00                      135.00!      Yes
    Quilts            700.00                       42.00!      No
    Wood Carvings     625.00                       37.50!
        Total       3,575+

Imports
    Toys            1,500.00                       90.00!      Yes
    Hats              850.00                       51.00!      No
        Total       2,350+                        474.00+

Quarter Total                   7,900.00=

Math                                          Doc 1  Pg 1  Ln 7      Pos 10
```

There are no decimal points for the totals in the first column, and the sales tax has been recalculated to reflect the new tax rate.

40.5 Enter the 2nd quarter figures

The final step in updating the financial statement is to include the figures for the 2nd quarter, then calculate.

MOVE To Line 26 Position 10.

↵ , ↑ Add a blank line, then move to the line.

Space Bar Press 3 times to indent the line.

TYPE **2nd Quarter**

Tab Press 2 times to insert two Tabs which move you to the Year to Date column.

TYPE **T6,950.00** for the 2nd Quarter Total.

Tab Insert a Tab which moves you to the Sales Tax column.

Back-space Delete the formula operator (!).

TYPE **t347.50** for the 2nd Quarter sales tax subtotal.

Alt F7 , 2 Select the *Calculate* option on the Math menu to calculate the edited financial statement.

```
        Quilts            700.00                        42.00!      No
        Wood Carvings     625.00                        37.50!
           Total        3,575+

     Imports
        Toys            1,500.00                         90.00!     Yes
        Hats              850.00                         51.00!     No
           Total        2,350+                          474.00+

     Quarter Total                    7,900.00=
        1st Quarter                   T3,275.00
        2nd Quarter                   T6,950.00          t347.50_

     Year to Date                    18,125.00*




     Math                                     Doc 1  Pg 1  Ln 26      Pos 68
```

40.6	**Print and save**

Now that you have edited the financial statement, you are ready to print and save it. Notice that the Math operators on the screen are not sent to the printer.

Shift F7 , 1 Select the *Full Text* option on the Print menu to print the financial statement.

F7 , Y Begin saving the financial statement.

ENTER **crafts.1** as the filename.

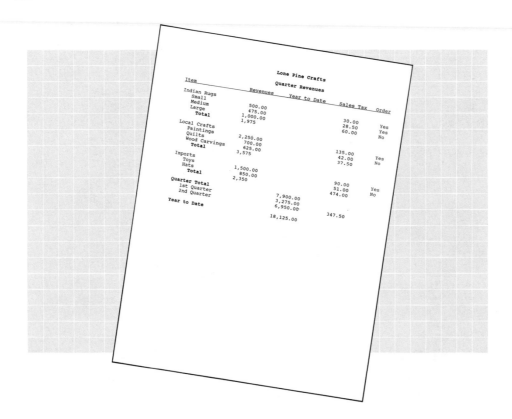 Clear the screen.

Lone Pine Crafts
Quarter Revenues

Item	Revenues	Year to Date	Sales Tax	Order
Indian Rugs				
Small	500.00		30.00	Yes
Medium	475.00		28.50	Yes
Large	1,000.00		60.00	No
Total	1,975			
Local Crafts				
Paintings	2,250.00		135.00	Yes
Quilts	700.00		42.00	No
Wood Carvings	625.00		37.50	
Total	3,575			
Imports				
Toys	1,500.00		90.00	Yes
Hats	850.00		51.00	No
Total	2,350		474.00	
Quarter Total				
1st Quarter		7,900.00		
2nd Quarter		3,275.00		
Year to Date		6,950.00		
		18,125.00	347.50	

Math Merge

WordPerfect lets you create math reports using information found in your secondary merge files. In this lesson, you add a numeric field to each record of a secondary file, then merge those fields into a math document.

While working through the lesson, you learn the following facts about WordPerfect's features:

- You can merge fields into a math document.

- After merging fields into a math document, you can then calculate totals using the new information.

The skills you learn in this lesson can be used to create reports (in a fraction of the time it would take to create the same report manually) regarding such varied information as:

- Grade point averages.
- Project man-hours.
- Equipment depreciation.

 ## 41.1   Edit the ADDRESS.SF file

Add a numeric field to each record in ADDRESS.SF, the secondary merge file you created in Lesson 9.

Shift F10   Select the Retrieve feature.

ENTER   **address.sf** as the filename.

```
Mr. Alan Wilson^R
Flatwood Market^R
55 E. Main Street
Flatwood, Utah 84999^R
801 666-4545^R
Alan^R
^E
Mr. Jeff Richards^R
Flatwood Motors^R
58090 Bonnie View Court
Flatwood, Utah 84999^R
801 666-6767^R
Jeff^R
^E
Mr. John Elliot^R
Wagon Wheel Diner^R
1100 North State Street
Flatwood, Utah 84999^R
^R
John^R
^E



B:\ADDRESS.SF                           Doc 1  Pg 1  Ln 1     Pos 10
```

MOVE To ^E in the last line of the first record (Line 7 Position 10).

TYPE **25,000** to add a numeric field to the record.

F9 End the new numeric field with ^R and return the cursor to the next line.

Now, add a numeric field to each record as illustrated in the following screen:

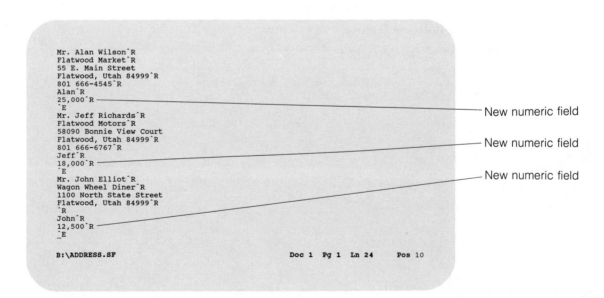

```
Mr. Alan Wilson^R
Flatwood Market^R
55 E. Main Street
Flatwood, Utah 84999^R
801 666-4545^R
Alan^R
25,000^R ————————————————————————————————— New numeric field
^E
Mr. Jeff Richards^R
Flatwood Motors^R
58090 Bonnie View Court
Flatwood, Utah 84999^R
801 666-6767^R
Jeff^R
18,000^R ————————————————————————————————— New numeric field
^E
Mr. John Elliot^R
Wagon Wheel Diner^R
1100 North State Street
Flatwood, Utah 84999^R
^R
John^R                                                         New numeric field
12,500^R ——————————
^E

B:\ADDRESS.SF                           Doc 1  Pg 1  Ln 24    Pos 10
```

F7 , **Y**   Begin saving the file.

ENTER   **address1.sf** to save this edited secondary file under a new filename.

↵   Clear the screen.

41.2   Set the tab stops

Set the tab stops for two columns in the math document.

Shift **F8** , **1**   Select the *Tabs* option on the Line Format menu to display the Tabs menu.

Ctrl **End**   Delete all existing tab stops (beginning at position 10) using the Delete EOL feature.

ENTER   **40** to insert a tab stop.

ENTER   **60** to insert another tab stop.

F7   Exit the Tabs menu.

41.3   Define the math columns

Because column A is already defined as a numeric column, you only need to change the definition of column B.

Alt **F7** , **2**   Select the *Math Define* option on the Math menu to display the Math Definition menu.

→ , **0**   Define column B as a calculation column.

ENTER   **1.1*A** as the calculation formula. This formula calculates a 10% increase of the value in column A. It could also be written as A+(.1*A).

F7   Exit the Math Definition menu.

1   Select the *Math On* option on the Math menu.

41.4   The primary file

Type and save the following primary file as SALARY.PF.

ENTER   **^F1^[TAB]^F6^[TAB][HRt]**
^N^P^P

Press the Enter key when you see [HRt], and press the Tab key when you see [TAB].

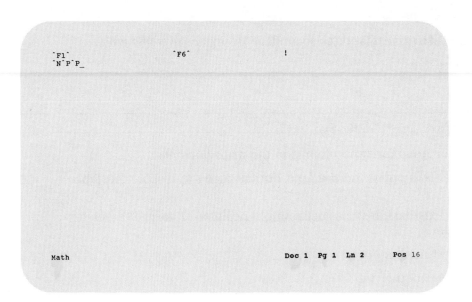

```
 ˆF1ˆ                    ˆF6ˆ                    !
 ˆNˆPˆP_




 Math                                    Doc 1  Pg 1  Ln 2      Pos 16
```

F7 , **Y**   Begin saving the file.

ENTER **salary.pf** as the filename.

↵   Clear the screen.

41.5 Start the merge

You are ready to merge into the math document and calculate the formulas.

Ctrl F9 , **1**   Select the *Merge* option on the Merge/Sort menu to start the merge.

ENTER **salary.pf** as the primary file.

ENTER **address1.sf** as the secondary file.

The merge begins.

Alt F7 , 2 Select the *Calculate* option on the Math menu to calculate the column.

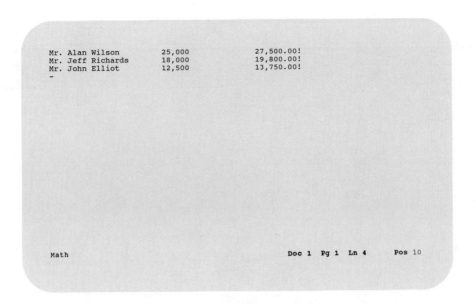

```
Mr. Alan Wilson        25,000          27,500.00!
Mr. Jeff Richards      18,000          19,800.00!
Mr. John Elliot        12,500          13,750.00!
-




Math                                    Doc 1  Pg 1  Ln 4      Pos 10
```

Index

P

^P	227,233
Page	
Center	25
Length	30
Numbers	62
Print	10
Page Numbering	
New	70
Restart	69
Paragraph	
Move	45
Numbering	137,141
Sort	206
Parallel Columns	78
Phonetic	60
Pitch	29
Primary file	86,223
Print	
Block	50
File	111
Full Text	20
Page	10
Printer, Merge to	226

R

^R	83
Redline	130,131
◀Release, Margin	80
Remove	134
Rename File	111
Repeating Macro Chains	188,196
Replace	67
Word	117
Reports and Lists	230
Restart Page Numbering	69
Retrieve Text	22,29
Return (Enter)	3
Reveal Codes	9
Right Justification	25

S

Save Document	11
Screen, Split	6
▶Search	31
And Replace	67
Name	33
Word	107
◀Search	255

Secondary File	83
Select	212,215
Select and Sort	
Double-Key	214
Multiple-Key	217
Single-Key	211
Sentence, Copy	48
Short Form	169
Simple Math	246
Single-Key Select/Sort	211
Skip Word	55
Sort	158,200
Line	199
Merge	209
Multiple-Level	203
Paragraph	206
Sort and Select	
Double-Key	214
Multiple-Key	217
Single-Key	211
Spacing	32
Change	63,65
Double	31
Spell-Checking	53
Speller, Start	54
Split Screen	66
Start	
Speller	54
Thesaurus	115
WordPerfect	4
Status Line	5
Strikeout	130,132
Subtotal	247
Switch	45

T

^T	227
Tab Stops	29
Table of Authorities	167
Table of Contents	145,146
Tables	147
Template, Keyboard	1
Text	
Columns	73
Lines	30
Thesaurus	115
Total, Grand	249
Troubleshooting	35
Typing	15

U

^U	233
Underline Text	15,44
Uppercase	45

V

^V	243

W

Window	66
Word	
Correct	55
Count	61
Search	107
Skip	55
Wrap	18
WordPerfect	
Exit	11
Start	4